WHAT PEOPLE ARE SA
WHEN CHRISTIANS ACT L

Have you ever wondered what would happen if Christians Acted Like Christians? Jeff Rosenau has thought deeply and wisely about this intriguing question. His persuasive new book provides the answer in a highly readable, engaging and convicting way. My recommendation – turn off your cell phone for a couple of hours and read this book. You'll be glad you did.

—William L. Armstrong
President, Colorado Christian University
United States Senator (1979-1991)

For those of us who want to be transformed so that by example we might restore peace in our own lives while improving our relations with others, Jeff Rosenau reminds us of God's call to Christlike civility. This practical book teaches us how and why we ought to follow Jesus' example as we enter every discussion with a firm conviction of Christian truth, a willingness to learn from those with whom we may disagree, and a desire to honor the humanity of even our fiercest foes. In a world where incivility and finger-pointing monologues are fast replacing Christlike dialogue, this book is needed more than ever.

—Samuel B. Casey
General Counsel, Advocates International,
Executive Director, Christian Legal Society (1994-2008)

Jeff has written a wonderful book that is well worth reading. His book is both wise and practical and should help the Christian community understand the beauty of Christlike civility. His message is strongly supported biblically. A great read.

—**Dr. Jim Dixon**
Senior Pastor
Cherry Hills Community Church

The most significant thing I can say about this book is the author lives the message God has given him to share. As Jeff points out, in most cases the relationship truly is more important than the issue and who happens to be "right". Giving up our right to be right is hard to do, even for Christians. Through Scripture and real life stories, this book conveys a convicting and inspirational call to a deeper level of maturity in Christ.

—**Dave Legg,**
Vice President, People Resources
The Navigators

Jeff Rosenau's insights into Christlike dialogue can change your life, help you maintain friendships when conflicts arise, and make friends out of enemies. The principles are sound. I once heard a quote attributed to Abraham Lincoln: "Do I not destroy my enemies when I make them my friends?" This book will help you do that.

—**Dr. David Osborn**
Director, Doctor of Ministry Program
Denver Seminary

WHEN CHRISTIANS ACT LIKE CHRISTIANS

—

God's Call To Christlike Civility

Jeff Rosenau

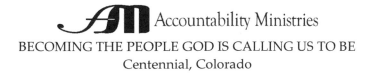 Accountability Ministries
BECOMING THE PEOPLE GOD IS CALLING US TO BE
Centennial, Colorado

Contents

PART FOUR

IS BOLDNESS CHRISTLIKE?

PART FIVE

JESUS MET NEEDS WITH GRACE AND TRUTH

PART SIX

BECOMING AN ANSWER TO GOD'S CALL

ACKNOWLEDGMENTS

Scripture, combined with the stories and thoughts presented in this book reflect insights God has graciously shared with me over the years, and it is my privilege to share them with you.

I praise God and give special thanks to my lovely wife, Candy. Not only has she been amazingly patient and supportive during the writing, organizing, and rewriting of this material, she has also spent numerous hours reading and editing this work. Her input and expertise have been a wonderful blessing.

I extend much gratitude to my friend, Wendy Shumaker for her excellent help with editing and organizing the manuscript during the initial stages of writing.

Most of all I praise God for the supernatural contribution of His Holy Spirit in helping to clearly articulate a message from a loving heavenly Father to His children. May God use the words in this book to transform many lives for His glory.

FOREWORD

Jeff Rosenau is part of the problem. So am I. So are you. Each of us finds it all too easy to think and speak in ways that hurt others and trigger conflict. Sometimes we do it knowingly, but more often we're oblivious to the way we're affecting others. We simply fail to act like Christians. In doing so, we weaken our relationships and damage our witness for Christ.

But Jeff is also part of the solution. In this invaluable book he shares profound insights into how God delights to transform our hearts and minds so we can engage others, even entrenched opponents, with Christlike gentleness and wisdom.

Jeff's insights and counsel beautifully mirror the timeless guidance given to us by the Apostle Paul in Colossians 3:12-15:

> Therefore, as God's chosen people, holy and dearly loved, clothe yourselves with compassion, kindness, humility, gentleness and patience. Bear with each other and forgive whatever grievances you may have against one another. Forgive as the Lord forgave you. And over all these virtues put on love, which binds them all together in perfect unity. Let the peace of Christ rule in your hearts, since as members of one body you were called to peace. And be thankful.

Like Paul, Jeff teaches that all real transformation begins not by doing, but by remembering. Remembering what God has already done for us: "the Lord forgave you." Remembering who we are in Christ: "God's chosen people, holy and dearly loved." Remembering what he has called us to: "as members of one body you were called to peace."

INTRODUCTION

I Was Part of the Problem

My journey began in 1993 as I listened to the secular media and Christian leadership quarrel over controversial issues of social and political concern. I sensed something was wrong in the way God's people were responding to people with opposing views. Was it the critical, self-righteous tone that I kept hearing, or was something else causing my concern? As it wasn't immediately clear to me what the problem was, I took time out to pray, "Father, there's so much wrong in our society and with Christianity, I have no idea what You would like me to do to help. But would You show me what's wrong with our society—what's wrong with Christianity—and what You would like me to do to help?"

God first introduced me to two secular organizations. The first one published guidelines for comprehensive sexuality education for public schools, kindergarten through twelfth grade. I ordered a copy of the guidelines and spent considerable time evaluating the content. As I read through them, I grew more aware of the agenda within those guidelines and how much I opposed the use of this material in the public schools. It seemed clear to me that the guidelines promoted abortion, homosexuality, and sex as a pleasurable and acceptable activity *outside of marriage.* From my perspective, it appeared that these guidelines were a thirteen-year package to undermine parental authority and any God-honoring influence within the public school system. For example, consider these two quotes from the *teaching guidelines for five-year-olds:*

Abortion is legal in the United States.

Sexual intercourse is a pleasurable activity for most adults.

As I shared the latter quote with a teacher one day, she replied, "Well, how would you want that to read?" I replied, "I would like it to read, 'Playing in a sandbox is a pleasurable activity for five-year-olds.' " She smiled and said, "So would I."

Next, God led me to a local non-profit organization that trained teachers in what was referred to as Comprehensive Health Education. This group promoted or endorsed six curricula; two for elementary-age students, two for middle school, and two for high school, each having a sex education component. I picked up copies of these curricula at several schools, then drove to the office of that organization for a copy of the one curriculum their organization had paid consultants to publish.

For the next several months, I conducted research on these national guidelines, and evaluated hundreds of pages of curricula that the state organization promoted or endorsed. I found that the philosophies of these two organizations differed little, if at all.

As this research drew to completion, I recognized that some very *unhealthy* guidelines about sexuality were being promoted within the public schools, guidelines that came across as being unopposed to promiscuity while indifferent to the option of sexual abstinence before marriage. Believing this material to be of great concern to God, I viewed the philosophy of this national organization as the Goliath of our day and was prepared to fight, failing to remember that "our struggle is not against flesh and blood" (Ephesians 6:12).

To meet this formidable challenge, I condensed and organized what I had learned from my research into a three-ring binder. It contained direct quotes from the national guidelines and curricula that I had evaluated. This helped to clearly expose agendas that I saw as detrimental to young people.

I began meeting one-to-one with the people who helped make decisions about what would be taught about sexuality in public school health classes. I spoke with teachers and the principal where my two sons attended high school. I went to other teachers, health coordinators, members of the Colorado State Board of Education, and Colorado legislators in an effort to simply share the truth and expose what was taking place. Most of these people, I found, would listen politely as we dialogued one-to-one. A few agreed to do what they could to make changes in what was being taught.

CONVICTION

During this two-year time period, I had worked closely with nine Christian abstinence educators in Colorado. They invited me to share my research publicly with larger groups of concerned citizens. I agreed to make two such presentations. However, during those talks I found myself to be critical and judgmental, not only of the national guidelines and state curricula, but also of the motives of the leaders within those sponsoring organizations. Gently, the Holy Spirit convicted me that the critical attitude that I was conveying to the audience was not the approach that God desired.

Shortly thereafter, I had occasion to meet with a good friend and one of my mentors, Don Reeverts, who was (and still is) president of the Denver Leadership Foundation. I would meet with Don occasionally to discuss my efforts at trying to bring about some God-honoring changes in sex education within the public schools. While Don wasn't opposed to what I was trying to accomplish, he expressed concern about how I was going

PART ONE

Am I Becoming
The Person
God Is Calling
Me To Be?

WORDS REVEAL HEARTS

In this book, we'll focus on communication and dialogue. Why? Because the words we speak reveal our hearts as Jesus taught us in Matthew 12:34, "For out of the overflow of the heart the mouth speaks." And just as Jesus addressed the hearts of people with His Sermon on the Mount, He encourages us to examine our hearts today.

The goal of this book is to help readers grow in their knowledge of the Son of God so that their personal relationship with Jesus will enable them to respond as Christ would to people of opposing views, producing a unique and uncommon civility that glorifies God.

We'll look to the Word of God to learn how He desires His children to communicate so that we bear witness unto His Son. But first, let's look at why we should even spend time doing this. Allow me to convey the need.

While presenting seminars to Christian audiences, I've asked the following questions: "Are God's children growing up into Christ? Are we reflecting His likeness when responding to people with opposing views? Are we becoming the people God is calling us to be?"

I then asked, "Which of the following forms of communication are most common among God's people:

- Gossip
- Quarreling
- Stereotyping
- Apathy/Indifference or
- Christlike Dialogue?"

From a survey of one thousand people, more than 95 percent acknowledged that gossip, quarreling, stereotyping, apathy or indifference are more prevalent among God's people than communicating through *Christlike dialogue* with one another.

As God's people, do we see a need to change our behavior? Is this how God intends His children to respond to people who disagree with us?

Even back in Paul's day, God's people had a reputation for ungodly communication. Listen to these words from Paul's letter written to Christians in the city of Corinth.

> For I am afraid that when I come I may not find you as I want you to be, and you may not find me as you want me to be. I fear that there may be quarreling, jealousy, outbursts of anger, factions, slander, gossip, arrogance and disorder. (2 Corinthians 12:20)

Our challenge comes through the words of Ephesians 4:15, "Instead, speaking the truth in love, we will in all things grow up into him who is the Head, that is, Christ." It would seem that for us to "grow up" into the likeness of Christ, we need to learn how to speak the truth to each other *in love* rather than as most of us have been doing it. It was clear to Paul that if we want to effectively bear witness unto Jesus to those around us, we need to choose our words carefully and intend for them to reveal love rather than discord.

UNDERSTANDING WHEREIN WE HAVE DEPARTED

Would you consider gossip to be speaking the truth in love? When we're quarreling with one another, are we speaking the truth in love—or maybe truth, but without love? How about when we stereotype others? Is being indifferent or avoiding conflict an expression of love?

Listen to these words from Dr. Henry Blackaby:

God's people do not even recognize that they have moved from what God wants them to be. So they're like Malachi, where God says, 'You've got to return to me,' and they say, 'Wherein have we departed?' Well look and see what is *not* happening because of a wrong focus by God's people. Are we going to be a people like God has asked us to be? Would we stop fussing within our churches? Would we stop fussing between our churches? Would we ask God to give us one heart and one mind and one soul? We've got to have an observable difference.

What might that look like; an observable difference — a people like God is calling us to be? Ephesians 4:13 reveals that it includes God's children reaching "unity in the faith and in the knowledge of the Son of God and [becoming] mature, attaining to the whole measure of the fullness of Christ."

The apostle Paul gives further instruction in Ephesians 4:29 on how we, as God's children, can have an observable difference, "Do not let any unwholesome talk come out of your mouths, but only what is helpful for building others up according to their needs, that it may benefit those who listen."

And a new command came from Jesus, that if obeyed will establish the defining characteristic of God's people, and set us apart from a secular world. That command from our Lord is, "Love one another. As I have loved you, so you must love one another. By this all men will know that you are my disciples, if you love one another" (John 13:34-35).

Are we known by our love for one another, or is unwholesome talk still coming out of our mouths?

Several years ago, as a seminary professor spoke to an audience of Christians, some liberal — others conservative, he asked them to share how they had stereotyped one another.

Listen closely to their responses.

HOW LIBERALS STEREOTYPED CONSERVATIVES:

- Close-minded
- Anti-intellectual
- Bigoted under the umbrella of Bible lingo
- Believing they have the only "right way"
- Political right-wingers
- Judgmental
- Literalists
- Militaristic
- Separatists
- More interested in a relationship with Jesus than in social justice
- Individuals who talk about God too much

Did you hear any wholesome words, words that would be helpful for building others up according to their needs?

HOW CONSERVATIVES STEREOTYPED LIBERALS:

- Wishy-washy
- Humanists
- Non-Christian
- Heretics
- Bleeding heart liberals
- Having no deep personal relationship with Jesus
- Relativists
- Evolutionists
- Pro-gay rights
- All Democrats
- Intellectual snobs
- Blind to sin

Did you hear any wholesome words—helpful for building others up according to their needs? Or did their response reveal how stereotyping, rather than *dialogue*, keeps us from having the kind of observable difference that draws people to Jesus Christ?

In addition to the absence of words that build others up, did you notice something else that was missing? *Love and dialogue*, without which our witness is compromised.

WILL WE ANSWER GOD'S CALL

As you read the words in the two lists, you may have found them to be somewhat humorous, as most of us do initially. They may be humorous to us because we can see ourselves making these comparisons. Here, too, we can see how our behavior needs to change. How easily we forget we have been forgiven by God, and that He wants us to extend the grace we have received from Him, to others.

I believe the clear, profound, and timely exhortation from our heavenly Father to us, His children, is: *It's time to grow up, into the likeness of My Son.*

If the words we speak are in need of change, we must first examine our hearts. So this book is less about learning how to communicate, than it is about *becoming the people God is calling us to be.* Rather than presenting a "how to" book or "steps to follow," this book offers a person to follow; namely Jesus Christ. For if we grow in our knowledge of Jesus and obey His teaching, we can discuss our differences with a *Christlike civility* that draws others to Him.

CHAPTER TWO

Is My Goal to Be "Right", or to Do Right?

If you really keep the royal law found in Scripture, "Love your neighbor as yourself," you are doing right.

—James 2:8

It takes God a long time to get us to stop thinking that unless everyone sees things exactly as we do, they must be wrong. That is never God's view. There is only one true liberty, the liberty of Jesus at work in our conscience enabling us to do what is right.

—Oswald Chambers, *My Utmost for His Highest*, May 6

INSTINCTIVE, OR TRANSFORMED?

Paul Tripp, in his book *War of Words,* wrote, "God is at work taking people who instinctively speak for themselves and transforming them into people who effectively speak for Him."

To gain understanding of the difference between instinctively speaking for ourselves and effectively speaking as Christ's ambassadors (2 Corinthians 5:20), consider the following two conversations.

The first conversation begins with two monologues and is a typical example of *instinctively speaking for ourselves.*

Let's set the stage. One of the participants in this conversation is a sixteen-year-old girl who is pregnant. She is not a Christian. Her boyfriend refuses to support her financially. Her parents are very upset and express their disappointment by refusing to help their daughter in any way. Distraught, and now contemplating abortion, she decides to first confide in one of her teachers, a woman who is a Christian.

The other participant in this conversation is the teacher, an *immature* Christian who believes it's her duty to convince this girl of the truth!

As they meet, the first conversation goes like this:

> **Girl:** "I just found out that I'm pregnant, and I need to talk with someone about it. I'm scared and don't know what to do. Would you have a few minutes?"

> Teacher: "What do you mean you don't know what to do? You should have the baby."

> **Girl:** "It's not that simple. My boyfriend doesn't want to marry me. My parents are very upset and

unwilling to help me financially. So I'm considering an abortion."

Teacher: "I don't think you should have an abortion."

Girl: "Well, what other options do I have?"

Teacher: "You should have the baby. Maybe your boyfriend will change his mind. If not, you can always put the baby up for adoption."

Girl: "I can't do that. Babies cost money and I don't have any. My parents won't give me a dime. I see abortion as my only option. I believe it's what's best for me, under the circumstances."

Teacher: "Don't you realize that you would be taking the life of an innocent unborn baby?"

Girl: "It's not a baby yet. It's nothing more than tissue."

Teacher: "That's not true. Listen to what the Bible says in Psalm 139:13-16."

Girl: "Why would I care what the Bible says. God doesn't care about me. If He did, I wouldn't be in this mess."

Teacher: "Don't blame God. You and your boyfriend should not have had sex until you were married. Don't you know what the Bible says about sexual immorality?"

Girl: "Hey, I came to you because you call yourself a 'Christian.' I thought you might be able to help me. But I'm sorry I did. You can save your preachin' for someone else."

CHANGING FOCUS AND MOTIVE

Regardless of what the issue may be in any disagreement, you will be faced with two choices:

1. Will you focus on the *issue*, or will you focus on the *relationship*?

2. Will you have a motive to *be "right" and to persuade someone to your point of view*, or will you choose a motive of *love for God and love for the other person*?

In the first conversation, the teacher was focused on the issue of abortion. Her motive was to persuade the girl to her point of view regarding abortion.

The second conversation is between the same two people, but this time it is a dialogue rather than two monologues. It helps us grasp what it means to *effectively speak as Christ's ambassadors*, when there is a new focus and a fresh motive.

The pregnant girl's circumstances have not changed. There is, however, a noticeable change in the Christian—she has been growing in Christ and has asked Him to teach her how to love those with whom she disagrees. Because of this change of heart, her response is quite different from what it had been.

During this dialogue, the Christian's *focus* is on building a relationship with this girl, rather than on the issue of abortion. The desire to have the girl see things exactly as she does has been replaced with a new *motive* to love this girl. Seeing more clearly from God's perspective, she now sees this young girl, not as opposition, but as a fellow human being who is hurting and in need of compassion. She becomes empathetic, trying to imagine what it would be like to be sixteen and pregnant, rejected by a boyfriend and parents, and left feeling unwanted, unloved, scared, and all alone.

She asks herself, "If I were in this girl's shoes, how would I want someone to treat me? How would Christ respond to her?" In this conversation, listen closely to identify ways in which the teacher now demonstrates *maturity in Christ*.

> **Girl:** "I just found out that I'm pregnant, and I need to talk with someone about it. I'm scared and don't know what to do."

> Teacher: "How can I help?"

> **Girl:** "Well, my boyfriend doesn't talk to me anymore. He won't even return my texts. My parents are really upset. They told me not to expect any help from them. But my friend, Heather, says she knows where I can have an abortion. I'm thinking about having it done."

> Teacher: "Have you considered all your options?"

> **Girl:** "I don't see any other option available to me. I can't afford a baby, and my boyfriend and parents won't help."

> Teacher: "There are people who do care and are willing to help you, including me."

> **Girl:** "How could you help?"

Teacher: "Would you mind if we first take a moment to pray and ask God to help us know what He would like us to do?"

Girl: "No, I don't mind."

Teacher: "Dear heavenly Father, I know how much You love this young girl and how much You love her baby. We are not sure what You want us to do, so we ask for Your wisdom and help. In Jesus' name, amen."

Girl: "What do you think I should do?"

Teacher: "Are you open to talking about possible options, besides abortion?"

Girl: "Yes, I'm open to hearing about them, but that doesn't mean I'll change my mind."

Teacher: "Have you considered adoption? Would you be willing to talk with someone who is a certified adoption specialist? I could arrange a meeting, and I would go with you if you would like me to."

Girl: "I haven't thought about adoption because I don't know how I could pay the expenses to even have the baby delivered."

Teacher: "If money was not a concern, would you be willing to keep the baby?"

Girl: "I would be more inclined to, but I know nothing about being a parent. I'm only sixteen."

Teacher: "I know of several centers and clinics that have people who come alongside and minister to women who experience unplanned pregnancies. Oftentimes, these are young girls like yourself who are considering abortion. The staff and volunteers at these organizations love those girls regardless of the choice they make. If they choose to keep the baby, they assist with financial support and classes on caring for a newborn baby, and managing a budget."

Girl: "I didn't know that, but I would like to learn more about them."

Teacher: "If you give me some days and times that you would be available to talk with them, I'll check their schedule, pick a date, and drive you there to meet them."

Girl: "You would do that for me?"

Teacher: "Absolutely, I would be honored to do that for you. And if you decide to keep your baby, you can count on me to be your friend and walk through this with you."

Girl: "Why would you do that?"

Teacher: "Because the love of my Savior, Jesus Christ compels me to love others as He has loved me. Do you know that Jesus loves you very much?"

Girl: "But what if I choose to have an abortion instead?"

Teacher: "Although I hope and pray that you will not choose to have an abortion, I want you to know that if you do, I'll still be your friend. While considering your options, I think you should know that serious consequences such as remorse, guilt, and physical complications are not uncommon to those who have chosen abortion."

"If you ever want to talk some more or pray together, come and see me. I will look forward to hearing from you regarding dates and times for us to visit my friends at the center."

I encourage you to read the two conversations again, this time to discover the difference between the words spoken instinctively by the Christian in the first conversation and her words in the second conversation as she practiced *dialogue in the Spirit of Christ.*

In the first conversation, you can sense that the Christian wants this girl to know the difference between right and wrong on the issue of abortion, as clearly as she sees it. But do you think the girl gets the impression that the Christian truly cares about her as a person and what she is struggling with? Though the teacher may have spoken words of truth, were they spoken in love? Did she communicate words of grace to a girl in need of compassion?

In the second conversation, a calm and peaceful tone exists that conveys sincere empathy for the young girl. The Christian communicates in a way that says to the girl, "What you are thinking, feeling, and believing matters to me." And it matters regardless of whether it is wrong thinking or right thinking. By asking questions and listening closely to this teenager's answers, the teacher demonstrates an *other-minded respect* for the girl. She doesn't tell her what to do, nor does she talk down to the girl in any way.

During the dialogue, do you think the girl felt loved, accepted and affirmed by the teacher? Did the words of the Christian communicate compassion, tenderness, and genuine concern for the girl? Did her responses indicate any desire to be "right," or was her motive to simply do what was right for this girl? During the entire conversation, did the Christian ever compromise truth in any way?

With a humble servant's heart, the Christian makes herself available to be this girl's friend, reassuring her that she is not alone. As the Christian speaks the truth in love, and points the girl to God through prayer, she provides opportunity for the girl to experience the love of Christ.

What Christians Must Learn

I believe that at least some of us are so focused on what others need to learn that we are neglecting to see what God may be asking *us* to learn. In short, before we can help others to see, we may still need to extract a plank or two from our own eyes. I honestly believe that, short of Christ's return, God will not bring an end to the abortion holocaust

---

until Christians learn all that *they* are meant to learn, namely, greater compassion for sinners.

—David C. Reardon, *Making Abortion Rare: A Healing Strategy for a Divided Nation,* p. 72

If you are about to communicate with someone who has an opposing view, is your desire to *be "right"*, or to *do what is right for God's glory*?

What is your primary motive for wanting to talk with that person?

When you meet, what will your focus be? What do you plan to devote most of your time and energy to discussing, and why?

Will you be speaking instinctively for yourself, or will you be effectively speaking as one of Christ's ambassadors?

REPENTANCE PRECEDES CHRISTLIKE CIVILITY

In the next two chapters, I identify two barriers that keep Christians from maturing in Christ and from becoming the people God is calling us to be.

The two barriers are *selfish ambition* and *busyness*. If we are guilty of this heart attitude and behavior, yet unwilling to repent of them, Christians will continue to:

- Fail at communicating with Christlike civility.
- Fail to replace gossip and quarreling with Christlike dialogue.
- Fail to have an observable difference from the world's way of responding to people with opposing views.
- Fail at being "salt" that gives people a thirst for knowing Jesus Christ.

CHAPTER THREE

———

Self-Centered, or Other-Minded?

Do nothing out of selfish ambition or vain conceit, but in humility consider others better than yourselves. Each of you should look not only to your own interests, but also to the interests of others.

—Philippians 2:3-4

As a pastor, I counseled married couples and could not solve their problems. The major problem I heard from wives was, "He doesn't love me." Wives are made to love, want to love, and expect love. Many husbands fail to deliver. But as I kept studying Scripture and counseling couples, I finally saw the other half of the equation. Husbands weren't saying it much, but they were thinking, *She doesn't respect me.* Husbands are made to be respected, want respect, and expect respect. Many wives fail to deliver. The result is that five out of ten marriages land in divorce court (and that includes evangelical Christians).

—Dr. Emerson Eggerichs, *Love & Respect*, p. 6

WHY OPPOSITES ATTRACT

Did you ever wonder why God designed opposites to attract in marriage? I believe the answer is to give us *practice*, practice at becoming more other-minded, and more like Christ in the process.

For this to occur in a marriage, each spouse must first become keenly aware of a primary need of their spouse. For the wife, that need is to be loved by her husband. For the husband, that need is for respect from his wife. That's why Paul wrote in Ephesians 5:33 that a husband "must love his wife" and a wife "must respect her husband."

SELFISH AMBITION PRODUCES QUARRELING AND MONOLOGUES

Following are two conversations. The first contains two monologues between two *self-centered* spouses. The second is a dialogue between a husband and wife who are becoming *other-minded*.

In this first conversation, it's a week before the couple's anniversary. The husband is busy at work and doesn't take time to consider where his wife might enjoy going for a romantic dinner. He thinks she will gladly help him choose a restaurant. As the conversation unfolds, listen closely to hear how both husband and wife fail to consider the needs of their spouse. Instead, their focus is on getting their own needs met.

The first conversation goes like this:

> **Husband:** "Honey, our anniversary is only a week away. I think we should go out to dinner and celebrate. Where would you like to go?"

> Wife: "I don't know. Where do you think we should go?"

Husband: "I don't know. I want to take you wherever you would like to go."

Wife: "I want you to decide."

Husband: "Okay, let's go to..." (and he names *his* favorite restaurant).

Wife: "I don't want to go there."

Husband: "Where would you like to go?"

Wife: "I don't know. Just not there."

Husband: "Well, how will I know unless you tell me?"

Wife: "Exactly. You wouldn't know unless I told you, but I'll bet you know the favorite restaurant of your clients at work, don't you?"

Husband: "What does that have to do with us and our anniversary?"

Wife: "I think you are more in love with your work than you are with me."

Husband: "I don't have a clue what you are talking about. I try to be thoughtful and ask where you would like to have dinner on our anniversary, and what do I get in return? Will you ever stop nagging me about my work? At least they appreciate me at the office."

Wife: "Why wouldn't they? You're sensitive to meeting *their* needs."

Husband: "That's the end of this conversation. I'm done talking."

Wife: "Yeah, big surprise. Run away from the problem, like you usually do."

In James 3:16, we learn that "where you have envy and *selfish ambition*, there you find disorder and every evil practice." And in James 4:1-3, *self-centered* motives are identified as the cause of fights and quarrels.

So to all husbands and wives who find yourselves facing a disagreement with your spouse, I encourage you to pray and ask God to reveal any selfish ambition within the heart of either person so that whoever is in need of repentance can do so prior to discussing your differences. For if either party has selfish ambition, you can expect two monologues, with an absence of communication that glorifies God.

OTHER-MINDEDNESS LEADS TO CHRISTLIKE CIVILITY AND DIALOGUE

The first Sunday following their argument, still wounded and distant, the couple quietly attends church together. During the sermon, the pastor's message is from Ephesians 5:22-33 regarding the roles of husbands and wives.

As the husband listens attentively, these words bring conviction to his heart, "Husbands, go all out in your love for your wives, exactly as Christ did for the church—a love marked by giving, not getting" (Ephesians 5:25, MSG).

Tears fall from his wife's eyes as she hears, "...and the wife must respect her husband" (Ephesians 5:33).

On their way home the husband says, "I'm sorry for failing to love you as I should. Will you forgive me?" His wife responds, "I do forgive you. And I'm sorry for failing to respect you as I should. Will you forgive me?" He replies, "I do." Then he adds, "When we get home I would like us to pray together and then discuss our recent argument to learn from God and each other how to become more *other-minded*."

When the couple returns home, they get on their knees and the husband leads them in prayer, "Father, I have sinned against You by not being obedient to love my wife in the ways Your Word teaches me to love her. I ask for Your forgiveness. Would You help me listen closely to better understand the needs of my spouse, and to become a more godly *other-minded* husband who communicates Christlike love to his wife?"

His wife adds, "Father, I am sorry for not being obedient to respect my husband as Your Word commands me to do. Please forgive me. I ask for Your help in becoming a more godly *other-minded* wife who communicates respect for her husband."

The second conversation is a Christlike dialogue between the husband and wife, who are now becoming *other-minded*.

> **Husband:** "I began our conversation by asking you where you would like to go to dinner to celebrate our anniversary. Why did you not perceive that to be an expression of my love for you?"

> Wife: "My thought was, if you loved me, you would know what restaurant I enjoy the most. I know you well enough to know that the restaurant you suggested is *your* favorite, rather than mine."

> **Husband:** "That's true. That was pretty inconsiderate

of me. Sadly, after you made the comment about me knowing the favorite restaurant of my clients, I realized that you were correct. But do you see how your statement that I am more in love with my work than with you came across to me as being disrespectful?"

Wife: "I do now that you have taken time to talk with me."

Husband: "I'm beginning to understand that I've been a crummy lover, but not because I don't love you. I love you very much. The problem has been that I've focused so much energy on getting *my need for respect* met through work, that I've neglected your need to be loved."

Wife: "I acknowledge that I have let you down in a similar way. My primary motive in our relationship has been to get *my need for love* met, and I've failed miserably at meeting your need for respect. But it has never been because I don't respect you. I do respect you, and I admire you immensely."

Husband: "My desire from this moment forward is to love you well, but I will need your help and God's help. I encourage you to communicate your needs to me. Will you help me understand when and how I fail to meet *your need* to be loved?"

Wife: "I will." "And just as you have expressed your desire for help in the area of loving me well, I ask for your help and God's help in knowing how to express my respect for you in ways that are pleasing and honoring to our God. When I'm disrespectful, will you please let me know?"

So you see that where one goes to dinner is far less important than how one communicates in the process of getting there.

REPLACING THE OLD WITH THE NEW

Self-centeredness produces quarrels, fighting, and disorder. It represents our old nature. *Other-mindedness leads to Christlike civility.* It reflects our new life in Jesus Christ.

If God's people are to become the people God is calling us to be, a people with an observable difference from the world, a people who bear witness unto Jesus Christ through the words we speak, our hearts must be cleansed of all selfish ambition so that the *other-minded life of Christ* shines through us.

While explaining to Christians how to practice biblical truths as they go about their daily lives, Paul included this exhortation in Romans 12:10: "Honor one another above yourselves."

In what ways are *you* honoring your spouse above yourself? How about with your children? People at work? At church? That person, or those people with whom you have disagreements?

CHAPTER FOUR

———

Too Busy, or Available?

As Jesus and his disciples were on their way, he came to a village where a woman named Martha opened her home to him. She had a sister called Mary, who sat at the Lord's feet listening to what he said. But Martha was distracted by all the preparations that had to be made.

—Luke 10:38-40

Where does the still, small voice of God fit into our hectic lives? When do we allow Him to lead and guide and correct and affirm? And if this seldom or never happens, how can we lead truly authentic Christian lives?

Authentic Christianity is not learning a set of doctrines and then stepping in cadence with people all marching the same way. It is not simply humanitarian service to the less fortunate. It is a walk—a supernatural walk with a living, dynamic, communicating God. Thus the heart and soul of the Christian life is learning to hear God's voice and developing the courage to do what He tells us to do.

Embarrassingly few Christians ever reach this level of authenticity; most Christians are just too busy. And the arch-enemy of spiritual authenticity is busyness, which is closely tied to something the Bible calls *worldliness*—getting caught up with this society's agenda, objectives, and activities to the neglect of walking with God.

47

No one can become an authentic Christian on a steady diet of activity. Power comes out of stillness; strength comes out of solitude. Decisions that change the entire course of your life come out of the holy of holies, your time of stillness before God.

—Bill Hybels, *Too Busy Not to Pray*, pp. 125-126, 147

GOING AFTER THE ONE LOST SHEEP

A pastor in Colorado shared a story with me regarding a marital conflict within his congregation that offers a challenging, yet inspirational reminder of what can happen if we slow down and make time for people. It provides an excellent example of how God intended church discipline to be administered as outlined in Matthew 18:15-17, with the ultimate goal being the restoration of the straying brother or sister, as gleaned from the parable in Matthew 18:10-14.

The couple came to church leadership for counsel. As the wife was shown her fault in the matter, she was quick to repent. However, the husband was not. So the elders took one or two others along to establish the facts. The husband remained unwilling to listen so they told the story to the entire congregation. Afterward, the unrepentant husband responded, "I don't care what you say. I'm going to divorce my wife and leave the fellowship."

Soon after, the man divorced his wife, left the fellowship, and moved to California.

But that wasn't the end of the story.

One of the elders who had been involved in that disciplinary process loved and cared enough about his brother in Christ that, at his own expense, he flew to California and made time to talk with the man.

Through that act of kindness, the previously unrepentant

brother broke down and wept. He became vulnerable and shared his weaknesses. He explained why he was hurting so much and why he had behaved so poorly. The man repented, moved back to Colorado, remarried his wife, and was restored to the fellowship.

This could happen a lot more, if we weren't *too busy*.

KNOWING TO WHOM YOU SHOULD BE AVAILABLE

When I read and think about Jesus' life, I picture an extremely diligent person, but I never see Him hurrying. What kept Jesus from hurrying, and from ever being *too busy*? How did He always know who to pass by, and who to stop for? Through the following quote, from page 96 of his book, *Spiritual Leadership*, J. Oswald Sanders provides some answers to those questions:

> Our Lord sets the perfect example of strategic use of time. He moved through life with measured steps, never hurried, though always surrounded by demands and crowds. When a person approached Him for help, Jesus gave the impression that He had no more important concern than the needs of His visitor.

> The secret of Jesus' serenity lay in His assurance that He was working according to the Father's plan for His life—a plan that embraced every hour and made provision for every contingency. Through communion in prayer with His Father, Jesus received each day both the words He would say and the works He would do. "The words I say to you are not just my own. Rather, it is the Father, living in me, who is doing his work" (John 14:10).

Conscious of time, Jesus spent His time doing things that mattered.

Jesus was always focused on relationships—with His Father and with people.

He preached to large audiences. He discipled a small group of twelve men for three years, was constantly teaching through word and by example, yet never neglected time alone with His Father in prayer.

He took time to listen and communicate with His enemies, the religious leaders of the day, though they didn't believe He was who He claimed to be. He made time to communicate and to build relationships through one-to-one dialogue with the Samaritan woman at the well, Nicodemus, Peter, and others. In each instance, He was about His Father's business informing people of who He was and of their need to know Him as their Savior and Lord.

Jesus made time to test a rich young man, and to gently communicate with some little children. He stopped to have dinner with Zacchaeus, show compassion for the woman caught in adultery, to hear and save the thief on the cross, to comfort Mary Magdalene upon His resurrection, convince doubting Thomas, and give hope to more than five hundred of the brothers before ascending into heaven.

How did Jesus *always* know His Father's will? Moving through crowds of people, yet stopping for only a few, how did He know who to stop for, and who to pass by? How did Jesus know how to respond—what to say and do—all in ways that glorified God?

He prayed.

Very early in the morning, while it was still dark, Jesus got up, left the house and went off to a solitary place, where he prayed. (Mark 1:35)

Jesus went out to a mountainside to pray, and spent the night praying to God. (Luke 6:12)

What about *you*? Are you too busy, or are you available to God and the people He wants you to stop and make time for? Are you spending enough intimate time alone with God in prayer to know who to stop for—how to respond—what to say and do—all in ways that glorify God, and then obediently being available to do so?

PART TWO

*From Immaturity
To Maturity*

CHAPTER FIVE

———

Transforming Power of the Holy Spirit

Now the Lord is the Spirit, and where the Spirit of the Lord is, there is freedom. And we, who with unveiled faces all reflect the Lord's glory, are being transformed into his likeness with ever-increasing glory, which comes from the Lord, who is the Spirit.

—2 Corinthians 3:17-18

What was Christ's relationship to the Spirit? Again, one of utter dependence. Nowhere do we read that Jesus performed any miracles or uttered marvelous teachings *before* His baptism and filling by the Spirit.

That simple dependence upon the Holy Spirit was necessary on Jesus' part for the accomplishing of God's will through Him. It is also necessary on *my* part if I am to accomplish God's will through me. God does not build His work on my personality, gifts, or abilities; He builds it on the Holy Spirit in me, with or without my abilities.

Jesus Christ, the Son of God, chose to let the Holy Spirit work completely through Him, and the "genius" aspect of Christ's life is simply the Holy Spirit doing the will of the Father through the obedient Son.

Victorious Christian living is not my "fulfilling myself"; rather, it is letting the Holy Spirit fulfill Himself in me.

—W. Glyn Evans, *Daily with my Lord*, August 20

REPLACING MIND OF MAN WITH MIND OF CHRIST

The most serious problem in the Corinthian church was worldliness, an unwillingness to stop being conformed to the culture around them. For this reason it was necessary for Paul to write to the Corinthians. Here's what he wrote in 1 Corinthians 3:1-3:

> Brothers, I could not address you as spiritual but as worldly—mere infants in Christ. I gave you milk, not solid food, for you were not yet ready for it. Indeed, you are still not ready. You are still worldly. For since there is jealousy and quarreling among you, are you not worldly? Are you not acting like mere men?

As the spiritual battle between good and evil intensifies, greater will be the need for spiritual maturity among God's people so that we respond as Christ would even in the face of persecution.

We mature spiritually as we "live by" and are "filled with the Spirit", rather than gratifying the desires of our sinful nature (Galatians 5:16; Ephesians 5:18). This means that throughout each day we choose to walk in the light of the Spirit's presence within us, allowing the mind of Christ to replace the thoughts of our old fleshly nature.

Our sinful nature provokes us to respond to people of opposing views with "hatred, discord, jealousy, fits of rage, selfish ambition, dissentions, factions and envy" (Galatians

5:20-21). As Christians, shouldn't we avoid and oppose such thoughts and actions?

On the other hand, when we choose to keep in step with the Holy Spirit, our responses will convey the fruit of God's Spirit, "love, joy, peace, patience, kindness, goodness, faithfulness, gentleness and self-control" (Galatians 5:22). Aren't these the attributes Christians should cultivate for God's glory?

In the following stories, three of Jesus' disciples—John, Peter, and Paul—respond to people of opposing views. First, they respond as mere men (worldly) gratifying the desires of their sinful nature. Later, they respond more like Christ (spiritually) *after having received and being filled with His Holy Spirit.*

FROM SON OF THUNDER TO APOSTLE OF LOVE
(John's Example)
As Jesus headed toward Jerusalem to celebrate the Passover, He was determined to complete His mission: to die on a Roman cross out of love for sinners. Jesus had sent messengers ahead of Him to prepare for His entrance into the city. But Jesus drew attention along the route from the residents of the Samaritan villages. The Samaritans were traditionally at odds with the Jews who opposed them, and the people at one of the villages did not welcome Jesus. "When the disciples James and John saw this, they asked, 'Lord, do you want us to call fire down from heaven to destroy them?' But Jesus turned and rebuked them, and they went to another village?" (Luke 9:54-56).

"Do you want us to call fire down from heaven to destroy them?" A response you might expect from two young men who Jesus had earlier given the name Boanerges, meaning **Sons of Thunder** (Mark 3:17).

Although the Samaritans did not know or worship the true and living God, Jesus' response was one of grace, rather than judgment. Christ's response to those who rejected Him exemplified a heart attitude that He longs for His followers to have.

Jesus continued His journey, eventually completed His mission, and ascended into heaven. Prior to His ascension, He took time to encourage and instruct His apostles with these words from Acts 1:4-5, 8:

> Do not leave Jerusalem, but wait for the gift my Father promised, which you have heard me speak about. For John baptized with water, but in a few days you will be baptized with the Holy Spirit.

> ...you will receive power when the Holy Spirit comes on you; and you will be my witnesses in Jerusalem, and in all Judea and Samaria, and to the ends of the earth.

So John, along with other disciples, waited and *was filled with the Holy Spirit*. Then, as an **Apostle of Love** (1 John 4:7-11), more intimately acquainted with the mind and heart of Christ, John returned with Peter to Samaria. On this trip, John would preach the gospel (Acts 8:25) to *save* the people, rather than call down fire to *destroy* them.

This same John went on to write one of the gospels and three epistles that bear his name. He was the person who sought to bring God's people back to the basics, the basics of belief in Jesus Christ, and obedience to His commands. This was the apostle who wrote in 1 John 2:24, "See that what you have heard from the beginning remains in you. If it does, you also will remain in the Son and in the Father," followed with clarification in 1 John 3:11, "This is the message you heard from the beginning: We should love one another."

What a difference in response when a person is filled with the Holy Spirit so that the *mind of man* can be *replaced with the mind of Christ*.

Think of ways in which you have responded to people with opposing views as a **Son of Thunder** (*worldly*, as a mere man or woman). Can you remember times when you have waited for and depended upon the Holy Spirit to communicate through you as an **Apostle of Love** (*spiritually*, as Christ)? How did the outcomes differ?

FROM FIGHTER TO PREACHER *(Peter's example)*

As Jesus explained to His disciples that He must suffer, be killed, and on the third day be raised to life, Peter takes Jesus aside and rebukes Him saying, "This shall never happen to you." To which Jesus replied, "Get behind me Satan! You do not have in mind the things of God, but the things of men" (Matthew 16:21-23).

Peter hadn't realized before the resurrection that Jesus' mission was to die as an atonement for our sins, according to "God's set purpose" (Acts 2:23). Therefore, we see another combative response from Peter when the soldiers and officers came to arrest Jesus at Gethsemane. In an attempt to prevent Jesus' arrest, Peter drew his sword and cut off the ear of the high priest's servant (John 18:10).

Again, Jesus admonished Peter to put away his sword and asked him the question, "Shall I not drink the cup the Father has given me?" (John 18:11).

Peter didn't understand that the cup Jesus referred to was God's wrath and judgment that Christ would bear on the cross as an atoning sacrifice for the sins of the whole world (1 John 2:1-2).

But when the day of Pentecost came, Peter, like John, received the Holy Spirit, and the mind of man began to be replaced with the mind of Christ. *Filled with the Holy Spirit*, Peter delivered a sermon with **Christlike boldness**, proclaiming **truth** to those who had just crucified Jesus (Acts 2:14-40).

About three thousand people came to a saving knowledge of Jesus Christ that day (Acts 2:41), but not because of Peter's eloquence or wisdom. The outcome was due to the divine power of the Holy Spirit working through Peter to touch hearts and transform lives.

With **Christlike humility**, Peter later wrote the following words of **grace** in 1 Peter 3:9,15:

> Do not repay evil with evil or insult with insult, but with blessing, because to this you were called so that you may inherit a blessing.

> But in your hearts set apart Christ as Lord. Always be prepared to give an answer to everyone who asks you to give the reason for the hope that you have. But do this with gentleness and respect.

This is the same Peter whose first response to opposition had earlier been the sword.

Because the Holy Spirit who lived within the hearts of John and Peter is the same Holy Spirit that lives within the hearts of all who believe in the Lord Jesus Christ, we too can communicate humbly, gently, and respectfully, while proclaiming the gospel boldly with a love for God that overflows onto those who don't yet know Jesus as their Savior and Lord.

If you're in the middle of a conflict with someone, in what ways do you find yourself trying to defend God using *man's ways*? List some ways in which *your* response confirms that you are allowing God to accomplish His primary purpose of saving and sanctifying people *His way*, through the words you have spoken to the opposing party?

FROM PERSECUTING CHRISTIANS TO PROCLAIMING THE GOSPEL *(Paul's example)*

Saul, later to be known as the Apostle Paul, is introduced within the New Testament as a persecutor of Christians. Raised as a Hebrew of the Hebrews, and a man of education and lineage, he's mentioned as present and consenting to the murder of Stephen, a Christian (Acts 7:59-8:1). Because of his hatred for those who believed in the Lord Jesus Christ, and his stature within the Jewish community, Saul had received a commission from the High Priest and elders in Jerusalem to imprison and punish followers of Jesus Christ (Acts 9:1-2). Much later, while speaking to a crowd in Jerusalem, Paul confessed that he had gone from one synagogue to another to imprison and beat those who believed in Jesus. And when the blood of Stephen was shed, Paul acknowledged that he stood there giving his approval and guarding the clothes of those who were killing him (Acts 22:19-20).

One day as he was heading toward Damascus to capture more followers of Christ, Saul was confronted by Jesus. This dramatic encounter had a life-changing impact upon Saul. He came to the sudden realization that he had been persecuting the Lord of all *truth* and His followers. Broken and distraught at what he had been doing, Saul repented and acknowledged Jesus as his Lord. The grace of God could not have been more obvious as this most unrighteous of men was forgiven and *filled with the Holy Spirit*. Miraculously, Saul was transformed **from being a persecutor of Christians into an evangelist who proclaimed the gospel for the remainder of his life.** Rather than going to synagogues to arrest Christians, he began to preach in the synagogues that Jesus is the Son of God, and proving that Jesus is the Christ (Acts 9:1-22).

With much gratitude and with a clear understanding of his new identity as a forgiven child of God, He passionately testified to the grace of God. In step with the Holy Spirit, he was inspired and used by God to write twelve books of the Bible including these words from Ephesians 4:31-5:2:

> Get rid of all bitterness, rage and anger, brawling and slander, along with every form of malice. Be kind and compassionate to one another, forgiving each other, just as in Christ God forgave you.

> Be imitators of God, therefore, as dearly loved children and live a life of love, just as Christ loved us and gave himself up for us.

What amazing power the Holy Spirit has to transform the lives of those who are willing to truly surrender to the will and ways of God, and who wait to be filled with and led by the Spirit of God.

Is your life being transformed? As you respond to people who wrong you, reject you, or disagree with you, listen to the words you speak. In what ways does *your* response reveal the mind and heart of the Son of God who lives within you?

CHAPTER SIX

Conflict Offers Opportunity

Instead, speaking the truth in love, we will in all things grow up into him who is the Head, that is, Christ.

—Ephesians 4:15

The touchy neighbor, demanding boss, touchy relative, controlling friend, unthankful child, and the unexpected accident are all tools of sanctification in the hands of our Lord.

—Paul David Tripp, *War of Words*, p. 80

WHAT IS SANCTIFICATION?

In his book, *My Utmost for His Highest* (February 8), Oswald Chambers explains:

> Sanctification means being made one with Jesus so that the nature that controlled Him will control us. Are we really prepared for what that will cost? It will cost absolutely everything in us which is not of God.

> The resounding evidence of the Holy Spirit in a person's life is the unmistakable family likeness to Jesus Christ, and the freedom from everything that is not like Him.

Were you aware that along that journey, God allows conflict into our lives as opportunity to conform us to the likeness of His Son? How, you say? By giving us practice at loving others as Christ has loved us, including love for those people who rub us the wrong way. It is in loving those who are hard to get along with (and perhaps that includes you and me), that we share in the sufferings of Christ as we experience how painful it can be to love someone who rejects you, or disagrees with your way of thinking. During that process, we get a tiny glimpse of the long-suffering of Christ in loving sinners like us.

A MISSED OPPORTUNITY

One day I received a telephone bill for our ministry, and noticed an error. I called the phone company, explained the mistake, and asked them to correct it. They said they would.

A month went by. I received another phone bill. The mistake had not been corrected. I called a second time. Calmly and politely I explained the error, and asked for it to be corrected. The person on the line assured me that the correction would be made.

Another month passed. The phone bill arrived without the anticipated correction. I was thinking to myself, *"Why can't these people get it right?"* I called again, and in a reasonable tone of voice explained that the error they twice said would be corrected, was still there. For the third time I was told it would be taken care of.

Thirty more days passed. And you guessed it. I got the bill, and the correction had not been made. The thought returned, *"Why can't these people get it right?"* During my next call, I responded in less than a Christlike way. When I finished, the woman on the other end of the line asked, "Didn't you say you work for a ministry?"

Having been immediately convicted, I replied, "Yes I did, and thank you for reminding me." I apologized to the woman for getting upset, and for not responding as I should have. We then had a cordial conversation as she shared that she and her husband also have a ministry.

The next time I received our bill in the mail, the correction had been made. And then the light bulb came on. *I was the one who wasn't getting it right.* God had given me another opportunity to respond as Christ would with patience and gentleness, yet I forgot and I failed to *practice* what Christ had taught me. To correct this, God used a fellow believer to hold me accountable.

That experience was a powerful reminder of our need to abide in Christ moment by moment so that we're never caught off guard and respond inappropriately, as I did.

Because God is gracious, He initially gives us practice through minor disagreements as I've described above. However, I believe His goal in giving us opportunities through conflict is ultimately to help us deepen our relationship with

Him so that we'll be prepared to respond as Jesus would, even when more serious trials and persecution come our way.

MUTUAL ACCOUNTABILITY

Besides maintaining an intimate love relationship with our Lord, we need each other. We need mutual accountability from another person or group of people if gossip and quarreling are to be replaced with conversation that is pleasing and honoring to our God.

I'm reminded of a time I taught a six-week class at our church for fifty middle-aged people, mostly married couples. I shared with them many of the biblical principles that are included in this book.

One Sunday, I asked them to look for opportunities throughout the week that would give them practice at responding as Christ would in the midst of conflict.

The following Sunday I asked if anyone had been given such an opportunity. One person raised his hand and explained that he had purchased a new computer, took it home and it didn't work. He took it back and was told they would fix it. The next day he picked up the "repaired" computer and returned home, only to discover that it still didn't work. He told us that at that point he was starting to get irritated and about to respond in a way that would express his displeasure, but then remembered the teaching the Sunday before, changed his mind, and responded more like he believed Christ would.

Another man, a young lawyer, explained that during a trial the previous week, the opposing attorney became very aggressive. He shared that he began to respond in kind, but remembered what he had learned in class the previous Sunday, and responded calmly.

"And I blew it this week," the young lawyer's wife

confessed. "I went to get some passports and discovered that I didn't have all the information they required. The woman at the counter was not helpful, and I didn't respond in the most Christlike way."

DO YOU HAVE AN ACCOUNTABILITY PARTNER?

Most of us are at risk of responding in the flesh (our old nature), rather than in the Spirit of Christ (our new nature) to people who keep us from getting our way, or those who become a hindrance to our lives going smoothly. Humanly speaking, it feels more satisfying to gossip or quarrel then to take the time to love someone. But we have a higher calling, and that is to be *conformed to the likeness of Christ*. When God allows people into our lives who irritate us in some way, the ensuing conflict offers us an opportunity to practice loving others as Christ has loved us. As His children, we know He is at work within us "to will and to act according to his good purpose" (Philippians 2:13), so that our character reflects that of Jesus.

Who are the people God has allowed into your life to give you such practice--a spouse? son or daughter? other relative? Maybe someone at church--a neighbor? employer? or fellow employee? Perhaps an atheist? a Muslim? or a person who favors same-sex marriages? Whoever the person might be, will they experience the *life of the Son of God in you* by your response to them? Will they perceive that you love and care about them more than you care about the issue or concern that divides you?

I encourage you to find a small group of people who are willing to hold one another accountable to replacing gossip, quarreling, stereotyping, apathy and indifference with *Christlike dialogue*.

Each time you meet, let each person in your group share opportunities God recently gave them to mature in Christ by responding as Jesus would to someone who disagreed with them, or wronged them in some way. Ask too, if they responded in a Christlike way. And if not, what action will they take to do what is right?

In the next chapter, we'll go deeper into what it means to love others as Christ has loved us, and to respond as Jesus would to someone you perceive to be undeserving of your love.

CHAPTER SEVEN

What Does Christlike Look Like?

[Jesus said,] "A new command I give you: Love one another. As I have loved you, so you must love one another. By this all men will know that you are my disciples, if you love one another."

—John 13:34-35

The Holy Spirit reveals that God loved me not because I was lovable, but because it was His nature to do so. Now, He says to me, show the same love to others—"Love as I have loved you." "I will bring any number of people about you whom you cannot respect, and you must exhibit My love to them as I have exhibited it to you."

The knowledge that God has loved me to the uttermost will send me forth into the world to love in the same way.

—Oswald Chambers, *My Utmost for His Highest*, May 11

LOVING OTHERS AS CHRIST HAS LOVED US

What can we learn from Scripture to remind us of some of the many ways in which Christ has loved us, so that we can practice loving others in similar ways?

I would like to give six examples. With each one, Christ sets the standard to which Christians should seek to be conformed, if indeed our goal is to mature in Christ for God's glory.

ACCEPT ONE ANOTHER

First, the Bible teaches that we are to "accept one another, then, just as Christ accepted you, in order to bring praise to God" (Romans 15:7).

Jesus is sinless. Jesus is the Son of God. Jesus is God incarnate. Yet He gave His life to bring sinners into His Father's family. And not only are they welcomed and accepted into His family, they are allowed to share in the inheritance of God's only Son.

So what does that say about a forgiven sinner who rejects or looks down upon a fellow forgiven sinner, instead of warmly welcoming and accepting each other in spite of any differences that exist?

Just as incompatibility exists within a natural family, it also occurs within the body of Christ. To be incompatible means to be opposed in character, and unable to live and work together in harmony. While there may be a natural tendency to focus on our differences, Jesus died so that our natural tendencies would be replaced with supernatural tendencies to view others from a divine perspective. God's will is for His children to experience a "spirit of unity" that glorifies Him (Romans 15:5-6).

As brothers and sisters in Christ, we are not opposed in character because God sees each of us as perfect *in Christ*, forgiven, loved, and accepted as members of His family.

Although true Christians are not opposed in character, it is important to remember that we are at different levels of spiritual maturity. And the mature acceptance of the immature ought to mark the attitudes and actions of followers of Jesus Christ, remembering our Lord and Savior's prayer "that we may be one" (John 17:20-23); one body of believers, with each member of the body dependent upon the other and working in harmony with one another, accepting each other in spite of our differences in order to bring praise to God.

In chapter twelve, verse eighteen of Romans, Paul provides a practical example of how Christians can model the grace of Christ to others with the words, "If it is possible, as far as it depends on you, live at peace with everyone."

Is there a brother or sister in Christ whom you have rejected in some way? If so, what action will you take to be accepting of that person, and to live at peace with them as much as it depends on you?

BEAR WITH AND FORGIVE ONE ANOTHER

Second, the Bible says, "Bear with each other and forgive whatever grievances you may have against one another. Forgive as the Lord forgave you" (Colossians 3:13).

Jesus epitomized what it means to forgive others. It matters not how small or great the sin, the blood of Jesus Christ, His death, burial and resurrection have made forgiveness of sin possible. Not only certain sins, but all our sins. Not just past sin, but present and future sin. Not only does He forgive, He forgets. He removes our sins "as far as the east is from the west" (Psalm 103:12) and He remembers them no more (Hebrews 8:12). He patiently bears with sinners, waiting for us to see our need for Him, not willing that any should perish. Why? Because His love for sinners like you and me is incomprehensible.

71

May we never forget that we are forgiven, yet always remember the cost of our forgiveness. And may the love of our humble Savior compel us to forgive others as He has forgiven us.

Is there someone you need to forgive? Are you patiently bearing with others, giving them time to repent and to mature?

LAY DOWN OUR LIVES

Third, the Bible teaches that "we ought to lay down our lives for our brothers" (1 John 3:16). Again, Jesus sets the supreme example by His self-sacrificing love. He loved people enough to lay down His life so that the lives of others could be redeemed. God calls Christians to the same standard of divine love for one another as His Son expressed to us. It is a love for the undeserving. It is a love for the unthankful. It is a love for the unlovable. It is not the kind of love that humans are capable of giving. It is the divine love of Christ flowing from within and through us as we become one with Him.

This kind of love may at some point include the laying down of our physical lives as it did for Jesus as well as all those who have been martyred because of their witness for Jesus Christ.

But while all of us will not be expected to lay down our physical lives, all of us do need to lay down our self-centered lives for our brothers and sisters. For if we can't be other-minded toward fellow Christians, how can the world expect to receive the love of Christ through us?

To become more like Christ, may we lay down our lives in any and every way that the Holy Spirit leads us to so that people will experience the love of Christ through us, and acquire a thirst to know Him better.

Is there someone for whom God is leading you to lay

down your self-centered life? In what ways can you express the other-minded life of *Christ in you* to that person?

SERVE ONE ANOTHER

Fourth, the Bible teaches that we are to serve one another in ways that Jesus taught and modeled for us (Matthew 20:25-28; John 13:1-17).

Worldly leaders seek power to control, rule, and place demands upon others with a prideful air of superiority over those under their authority. Jesus, on the other hand, left heaven to come to earth. He came not to judge, not to dictate, nor to manipulate, but to serve.

The night before He would be betrayed, Jesus took time to wash His disciples' feet, including the feet of Judas Iscariot, knowing Judas would betray Him. Why would the leader of these twelve men choose to perform an act that was normally reserved for lowly menial servants? Why didn't Jesus ask or demand that His disciples wash His feet, instead of Him washing theirs? Because Jesus was a *humble servant-leader*. Once again, He set the standard of perfection for His followers.

He washed their feet to symbolize the value of spiritual washing and cleansing of souls from the defilement of sin. Those who have received such cleansing do well to remember the example the Lord set in the upper room following the last supper.

Serving others was Jesus' method and style of leadership. His approach was not to be arrogant, controlling, and oppressive in ways that demanded people to follow Him. Instead, His approach was to be diligent in prayer, to be available to people, to listen well, to teach the Word of God boldly, to heal the sick, to do good, to do right, to mentor and disciple others, to suffer silently and patiently, and then to die so that others might live.

Christian leaders who put into practice what Jesus taught us by His example will bring glory to God. If you are a person in authority, what changes do you think God would like you to make in order to become the kind of *servant-leader* He is calling you to be?

BE WILLING TO SUFFER INJUSTICE

Fifth, the Bible teaches us that Christ was willing to suffer injustice out of love for us (Isaiah 53; 1 Peter 2:21-24; 4:1-2).

The Son of God—King of kings—Lord of lords—the true and living God incarnate hung upon the cross. He was the Suffering Servant that Isaiah prophesied would come, the perfect model of how to respond to injustice and unjust suffering.

Just think of being betrayed by someone you have mentored, discipled, and loved for several years, followed by close friends deserting you, with one denying ever having known you, then left alone to be mocked, insulted, humiliated, whipped, beaten, scourged, and to have sharp thorns cut into your head, knowing the pain and suffering has just begun.

Next you are laid upon two long narrow pieces of rough wood. Your arms are stretched out and you see a Roman soldier with a large hammer and a long spike. Near your hand and wrist, you feel the sharp end of the spike and watch as the soldier's arm swings down forcefully. The spike crushes through your flesh. More pain is endured as another nail is driven through your other hand. A soldier grabs your feet and crosses one over the other. You feel the next nail touch the top of your foot, knowing it will likely penetrate through bone if it's to be securely fastened to the wood. Again, you see the soldier's arm swing forward, and wince when the blow is delivered. And as the cross is raised, you are left to die the slow and agonizing death that accompanies crucifixion.

Now imagine having to endure this suffering when you are completely innocent—absolutely sinless—and without fault of any kind.

How would you respond?

How did Jesus respond, the One whose example we are to follow? He suffered with perfect patience. He never expressed any anger. He did not open His mouth to speak harsh words or raise His voice with vengeful threats. "When they hurled their insults at him, he did not retaliate; when he suffered, he made no threats. Instead, he entrusted himself to him who judges justly" (1 Peter 2:23).

Jesus entrusted Himself to His Father with perfect peace and confidence, knowing that His suffering, death, and resurrection were required for the salvation of souls.

When Jesus did open His mouth, it was to save, to forgive, and to care for family. He promised salvation to one of the thieves hanging on a cross next to Him. He looked out at the crowd and asked His Father to forgive them for what they had done to Him. He saw His mother and John, one of His disciples standing below. He said to His mother, "Dear woman, here is your son," and to the disciple, "Here is your mother" (John 19:26-27).

What extraordinary other-mindedness from someone who is suffering and dying on a cross.

Christ's example should inspire us, understanding that the freedom we now have from sin and the gift of eternal life in heaven were made possible because of Christ's love, humility, and willingness to respond in obedience, knowing He would die as He did.

Christ's sinlessness made Him an unblemished sacrifice, acceptable and pleasing to God. Likewise, it's important for us to be innocent both in attitude and behavior if our patient endurance of sufferings is to be valuable in God's sight and provide effective testimony before men. As we yield our lives to God and His ways, demonstrated by a Christlike response when suffering injustice, others can experience the amazing grace of God.

Has the love of Christ compelled you to live your life on earth pursuing the holy will of God, rather than the self-centered ungodly lusts of the flesh? Are you as surrendered as Christ was to doing the will of our heavenly Father, whatever the cost? Will your response to people who disagree with you make it clear that you are willing to share in the sufferings of Christ and entrust yourself to the One who judges justly?

EXTEND GRACE, KINDNESS AND MERCY TO OTHERS

Sixth, the Bible teaches us that God our Savior has loved us by extending grace and kindness in order to save us, "not because of any righteous things we had done, but because of his mercy" (Titus 3:5).

Far from being righteous, we "were foolish, disobedient, deceived and enslaved by all kinds of passions and pleasures. We have lived in malice and envy, being hated and hating one another" (Titus 3:3). Like Adam and Eve after they disobeyed God, we too were dead in our transgressions and sins, and we were by nature, objects of God's wrath (Ephesians 2:1-3).

How does our God and Savior respond to such sinners who at some point repent and believe in the Lord Jesus Christ? Because of His grace, mercy and kindness, here are some of the ways:

- God "saved us through the washing of rebirth and renewal by the Holy Spirit" (Titus 3:5).

- God "made us alive with Christ, even when we were dead in transgressions" (Ephesians 2:5).

- "God made him [Jesus] who had no sin to be sin for us, so that in him we might become the righteousness of God" (2 Corinthians 5:21).

- God adopts us as His children, and we become "heirs of God and co-heirs with Christ" (Romans 8:17).

- "God raised us up with Christ and seated us with him in the heavenly realms in Christ Jesus" (Ephesians 2:6).

- God promises us eternal life with Him (John 3:16; 1 Peter 1:3-4; 1 John 5:11-13).

What should take place in the lives of those who receive such undeserved blessings from a gracious God? Shouldn't we see a transformation that produces a more Christlike disposition?

Listen to the following quote to remember that God has always been about the business of transforming the lives of sinners for His glory.

The great missionary Hudson Taylor said, 'All God's giants were weak people.' Moses's weakness was his temper. It caused him to murder an Egyptian, strike the rock he was supposed to speak to, and break the tablets of the Ten Commandments. Yet God transformed Moses into *'the humblest man on earth'* (Numbers 12:3). Gideon's weakness was low self-esteem and deep insecurities, but God transformed him into a *'mighty man of valor'* (Judges 6:12, KJV). Abraham's weakness was fear. Not once, but twice, he claimed his wife was his sister to protect himself. But God transformed Abraham into *'the father of those who have faith'* (Romans 4:11, NLT). Impulsive, weak-willed Peter became *'a rock'* (Matthew 16:18, TEV)...

—Rick Warren, *The Purpose Driven Life*, pp. 275-276

What made the transformation of these lives possible? The love of God expressed through His grace, kindness and mercy to sinners.

Perhaps God has placed a sinner into your life to give you practice at loving that person as Christ has loved you, with grace, kindness and mercy. Maybe you view that person as being undeserving of your love. Maybe they are. That's why it's called grace.

The question isn't whether someone is deserving of your love. The real question is, "Are you willing to obey Jesus' command to love others as He has loved you?"

FOLLOWING CHRIST'S EXAMPLE

In summary, here are some ways Christians can practice loving others as Christ has loved you:

1. Accept one another.
2. Bear with and forgive each other.
3. Lay down our lives for our brothers and sisters.
4. Serve one another.
5. Be willing to suffer injustice.
6. Extend grace, kindness and mercy to others.

Please keep in mind that the above is not a "to do" list to accomplish in your own strength. Instead, the power to love the undeserving and unlovable in these ways comes from the

Holy Spirit living within us, enabling us to love others with the supernatural love of Christ when we trust God enough to respond in obedience to His will and ways.

To catch a glimpse of what it means to put these teachings into practice in order to love others as Christ has loved you, listen closely to the following story.

A Love That Would Not Give Up

At the very least, actively loving an enemy will protect you from being spiritually defeated by anger, bitterness, and a thirst for revenge. And, in some cases, your active and determined love for your opponent may be used by God to bring that person to repentance.

This power was vividly demonstrated during World War II by a Catholic priest named Hugh O'Flaherty, who served in the Vatican during the war. As he learned of Nazi atrocities, he became actively involved in efforts to protect the Jews and to hide Allied pilots who had been shot down over Italy. Colonel Kappler; the German SS commander in Rome, eventually learned of O'Flaherty's activities and set out to kill him. Several assassination attempts failed, but Kappler finally succeeded in capturing several of O'Flaherty's associates. Kappler himself ordered the torture and execution of these prisoners, one of whom was O'Flaherty's closest friend.

When the Allied armies invaded Italy and surrounded Rome in 1944, Colonel Kappler was captured. He was sentenced to life imprisonment for his war crimes. In spite of all the wrongs Kappler had committed, O'Flaherty resisted the temptation to delight in his enemy's downfall. Instead, remembering Jesus' teaching and example, O'Flaherty resolved to love his enemy not only with words, but also with actions. Every month, he drove

---

to Gaeta Prison to see the man who had tried so hard to kill him. Year after year he learned about Kappler's needs and did all he could to meet them. Above all else, he demonstrated to Kappler the love, mercy, and forgiveness of God. In March of 1959, after almost 180 visits from the priest, Kappler finally confessed his sins and prayed with the priest to accept Christ as his Savior.

—Ken Sande, *The Peacemaker*, pp. 202-203

O' Flaherty made 180 visits to Gaeta Prison, once every month. That's a total of fifteen years (1944-1959) of being faithful to love someone who tried to kill him. What a powerful testimony of what it means to love the unworthy as Christ has loved us.

Do *you* trust God enough to love others as Christ has loved you?

PART THREE

Maturity In Christ Requires Meekness

CHAPTER EIGHT

The Meek Surrender, But Never Lose

And the Lord's servant must not quarrel; instead, he must be kind to everyone, able to teach, not resentful. Those who oppose him he must gently instruct, in the hope that God will grant them repentance leading them to a knowledge of the truth, and that they will come to their senses and escape from the trap of the devil, who has taken them captive to do his will.

—2 Timothy 2:24-26

High on my list of favorite Scriptures are Jesus' words in Matthew 11:28-30: "Come to me, all you who are weary and burdened, and I will give you rest. Take my yoke upon you and learn from me, for I am gentle and humble in heart, and you will find rest for your souls. For my yoke is easy and my burden light." What does He mean, to take His yoke? Where is rest hiding?

The answer lies in meekness. In this passage, Christ calls Himself "gentle and humble"—meek. He came not to judge but to die. He came not to shout and defend the honor of the Father but to die. He came not to fight but to die. No persecution could disturb Him for He came to suffer. Yet all the time He was suffering, He knew He was winning.

We, too, can suffer and win. We can live with love even when others hate—all the time knowing that love wins. We can respond with grace when others fight, knowing that grace wins. When we come to Him and surrender, accepting His yoke, we accept full vulnerability to the onslaught of the world. Yet, at the same time, we are assured that nothing can separate us from the victorious love of Christ. This rest is a self-weakening unto God-strength. It is a self-emptying unto God-fullness. It is the rest of full surrender.

Jesus calls us to His rest, and meekness is His method.

—Richard A. Swenson, M.D., *Margin*, pp. 233-234

OUR JOB—GOD'S JOB

When it comes to our responses to people with opposing views, three ways of proving our willingness to take Jesus' yoke and learn from Him will come by way of our obedience to Paul's instructions found in 2 Timothy 2:24-25. In that passage of Scripture, Paul informs us that *our job* consists of the following three "musts":

1. We must not quarrel.
2. We must be kind to everyone.
3. We must gently instruct others.

Why? Because these Christlike responses release the power of the Holy Spirit to change hearts and transform lives for God's glory.

God's job is to grant repentance (if He chooses to after examining a person's heart) and then lead whoever is deceived "to a knowledge of the truth" (2 Timothy 2:25).

When you're in a conflict, ask yourself, "Do I have the love of Christ for this person? Do I have concern for Christ's interests and the spiritual well-being of the person who opposes me?" Or do I simply have anger and resentment toward him because he is getting in the way of my self-interests, and/or doesn't see things exactly as I do?

A WORD TO CHRISTIAN POLITICAL ACTIVISTS

One day I was presenting a seminar to an audience of Christian political activists. During our time together, I shared a concern that I perceived to be a barrier to their effectiveness in bringing about change that could benefit society. I explained that, in certain instances, some Christian activists communicated in ways that revealed they not only expected non-Christian opponents to live righteous lives, but in some sense even demanded they do so. Yet they were not willing to share Christ with those people.

So to all my brothers and sisters in Christ serving as Christian political activists, I present these questions for you to prayerfully consider.

1. Do you have unrealistic expectations of someone who isn't a Christian, demonstrated by your anger directed at that person's unwillingness to do what is "right"?

2. If yes, are you willing to share Jesus Christ with them?

3. If they do not know Jesus as their personal Savior, and you are not willing to proclaim the gospel to them in a Christlike way, how righteous of a life should you expect them to live, and what spiritual truths should you expect them to comprehend?

To those who recognize and acknowledge they have fallen short of responding to opposition in ways that glorify God, I encourage you to practice *Christlike civility* when responding to and communicating with people of opposing views—people you may perceive to be your enemy—yet people God has allowed into your life for a reason.

As you talk with non-Christians who disagree with you about social or political concerns, would you ponder these words from Paul in 1 Corinthians 2:14?

> The man without the Spirit does not accept the things that come from the Spirit of God, for they are foolishness to him, and he cannot understand them, because they are spiritually discerned.

Prior to talking with your opponent, will you set a goal for yourself to grow in your knowledge of Jesus while you discuss your differences? Will you pray and ask God to help you respond to that person as Christ would? If the opposing party is not a Christian, are you open to sharing the gospel with the person as the Holy Spirit leads you to? And will you pray for that person's salvation?

If God uses your witness to bring that person to a saving knowledge of His Son, God will have accomplished a kingdom purpose through you. In addition, there is a good likelihood that you will have gained a friend and ally in the process.

Even if your concern is legitimate, we must never forget how patient God has been with us so that we do not become impatient with others.

While we must never stop doing what is right, let us remember that others may not yet have the spiritual power to do so.

WILL YOU SURRENDER?

If you are currently in the midst of a disagreement with someone, and desire to know if you are willing to take Jesus' yoke and learn from Him, ask yourself these three questions:

1. Am I refraining from quarreling with this person?
2. Am I being kind to this human being?
3. Am I gently instructing this individual?

As you pray about how you can obey the three "musts" of 2 Timothy 2:24-25, remember: *the meek surrender, but never lose.*

While you reflect and pray, may the words that follow help us to never forget the victory Christ won for us because of His willingness to surrender.

The Power Of Lamb-Likeness

We may well ask what gives the Blood its power!

Not the Blood of the Warrior, but the Blood of *the Lamb!* In other words, that which gives the precious Blood its power with God for men is the lamb-like disposition of the One who shed it.... But the title "the Lamb" has a deeper meaning. It describes His character. He is the Lamb in that He is meek and lowly in heart, gentle and unresisting, and all the time surrendering His own will to the Father's for the blessing and saving of men. Anyone but the Lamb would have resented and resisted the treatment men gave Him. But He, in obedience to the Father and out of love for us, did neither. Men did what they liked to Him and for our sakes He yielded all the time. When He was reviled, He reviled not again. When He suffered, He threatened not. No standing up for His rights, no hitting back, no resentment, no complaining! How different from us! …the nailing and the lifting up, the piercing of His side and the flowing of His Blood—none of these things would ever have been, had He not been the Lamb. And all that to pay the price of *my* sin! So we see He is not merely the Lamb because He died on the Cross, but He died upon the Cross because He is the Lamb.

Let us ever see this disposition in the Blood. Let every mention of the Blood call to mind the deep humility and self-surrender of the Lamb, for it is this disposition that gives the Blood its wonderful power with God. Humility, lamb-likeness, the surrender of our wills to God, are what He looks for supremely from man.

—Roy Hession, *Calvary Road*, pp. 98-101

CHAPTER NINE

Why Arguing May Be Okay, But Quarreling Isn't

And the Lord's servant must not quarrel.

—2 Timothy 2:24

A number of books have been written about evangelicals losing their influence in society. These books focus on the lack of biblical thinking about what's going on in our society. But a lack of biblical thinking is not the only problem. One of the leaders of this movement is a seminary professor who refuses to speak to the president of his institution because he disagrees with some of the policies that the president and the board have decided upon.

While biblical thinking is important, so is biblical *living*. The crisis of Christians in our society is not so much in the way we think about Christianity but in the way we live it out.

—John Vawter, *Uncommon Graces*, pp. 116-117

DIFFERENCE BETWEEN ARGUING AND QUARRELING

The *Oxford American Dictionary* includes the following definitions for the words, "argue" and "quarrel":

Argue   To give reasons for or against something, to debate.

Quarrel   A violent disagreement, breaking of friendly relations.

In regard to arguing, it can be okay when it's simply a formal discussion of a particular issue or matter of concern. But not all arguing is okay, as Paul points out to us in 2 Timothy 2:23 with the words, "Don't have anything to do with stupid and foolish arguments, because you know they produce quarrels."

How would you define a stupid and foolish argument? Write down a few examples of instances you have experienced or heard about in which arguments have led to strife and division within a congregation, between denominations, at home, or in the workplace.

At the point of disagreement when one or both parties begin to break off friendly relations with one another, the discussion moves from arguing to quarreling. *And the Lord's servant must not quarrel.*

Once you begin to have feelings of resentment toward someone who has an opposing view, beware! At that point, you are at risk of focusing more on the issue than the relationship and your motive to be "right" takes priority over the motive of love for the other person. If Satan can cause you to have bitterness and hatred toward another person, he's won and you have failed to bear witness unto Jesus Christ.

Remember, Jesus' motive was love for the people he spoke to. For us to love others with the love of Christ in the midst of conflict, shouldn't we begin by presenting a Christlike example through the words we speak to disagreeable people?

CHAPTER TEN

Be Kind to Whom?

And the Lord's servant...must be kind to everyone.

—2 Timothy 2:24

Let our temperament be under the control of the love of Jesus: *He can* make us gentle and patient. Let the vow that not an unkind word about others shall ever be heard from our lips be laid trustingly at His feet. Let the gentleness that refuses to take offense, that is always ready to excuse, and to think and hope the best, mark our behavior with everyone.

— Andrew Murray, *Abiding in Christ*, p. 161

knowledge of His Son, and to respond as He would to people who don't see things exactly as I do. That, together with the fact that the insurance supervisor had forewarned me that the insured was upset, kept me from being caught off guard. I was given time to prepare my heart and mind to go in the Spirit of Christ.

But what if I hadn't been forewarned? Instead, let's say my sons and I had planned a typical day of adjusting property claims, with ten appointments scheduled, allowing roughly one hour per claim, including travel time between claims and the writing up of reports. Listen as this day unfolds.

The first half is going smoothly. Five claims have been adjusted, and we're right on schedule. But now we come to the sixth claim, and are unexpectedly confronted with the gentleman referred to earlier.

Would I have been as *patient*, knowing we have four more appointments? Would I have been as *kind*, knowing that people might get upset if we're late or need to reschedule?

Would I have responded as Christ with the fruit of His Spirit, or might I have responded in the flesh by being impatient and unkind?

The answer would be determined by my decision for that day and that moment, whether or not to be abiding in Christ and walking in His Spirit, prepared to respond with the heart and mind of Jesus.

What about *you*? You have now been forewarned that God likely will at some point in your life (if He hasn't already) allow someone into your life who you will perceive to be unreasonable in some way. Will you be walking close enough with Christ to respond with the fruit of His Spirit, or will you be at risk of using words that would be displeasing to God and not reflective of His character? What action will you take to prepare yourself for such an encounter?

CHAPTER ELEVEN

Why Are We to Respond Gently?

Those who oppose him, he must gently instruct.

—2 Timothy 2:25

What Gentleness Means

In our rough-and-rugged individualism, we think of gentleness as weakness, being soft, and virtually spineless. Not so! The Greek term is extremely colorful, helping us grasp a correct understanding of why the Lord sees the need for servants to be gentle.

It is used several ways in extra-biblical literature:

- A wild stallion that has been tamed, brought under control, is described as being "gentle."
- Carefully chosen words that soothe strong emotions are referred to as "gentle" words.
- Ointment that takes the fever and sting out of a wound is called "gentle."
- In one of Plato's works, a child asks the physician to be tender as he treats him. The child uses this term "gentle."
- Those who are polite, who have tact and are courteous, and who treat others with dignity and respect are called "gentle" people.

So then, gentleness includes such enviable qualities as having strength under control, being calm and peaceful when surrounded by a heated atmosphere, emitting a soothing effect on those who may be angry or otherwise beside themselves, and possessing tact and gracious courtesy that causes others to retain their self-esteem and dignity. Clearly, it includes a Christlikeness, since the same word is used to describe His own makeup:

> Come to Me, all who are weary and heavy-laden, and I will give you rest. Take my yoke upon you and learn from Me, for I am gentle and humble in heart; and YOU SHALL FIND REST FOR YOUR SOULS (Matthew 11:28-29, NASB).

—Charles R. Swindoll,
Improving Your Serve, pp. 104-105

HARSH WORDS VS. GENTLE INSTRUCTION

In Proverbs 15:1, Solomon wrote the words, "A gentle answer turns away wrath, but a harsh word stirs up anger." In the following scenario a father and his eighteen-year-old son have a difference of opinion. In the first conversation, observe how harsh words stir up anger. Note the change in outcome when gentleness is practiced in the second conversation.

The son, away at his first year of college calls home and asks his father what he thinks about him getting a tattoo. The father tries to discourage his son from getting a tattoo, then both drop the subject. A couple of weeks later, the son comes home for spring break sporting a new tattoo.

HARSH WORDS

The first conversation involves two monologues. The scenario unfolds as the son's car pulls into the driveway. The father is at the front door to greet him, but as he spots the tattoo, his smile turns to a scowl. He is very upset, and responds harshly. His son becomes defensive.

> **Father:** "Well look at you! I thought I told you not to get that tattoo. What's wrong with you?"

> Son: "Dad, all my friends have one. We don't see anything wrong with it."

> **Father:** "Well, your generation doesn't see a lot of things that are wrong. When I was your age, none of my friends or I ever had a tattoo. "

> Son: "Maybe so, but your generation did a lot of other things that were wrong. If your generation hadn't been so messed up, maybe ours wouldn't be either."

> **Father:** "You don't talk that way to me, young man. The bottom line is that if you're going to live in this house, you'll live by my rules. I'm the one who's paying for your college. Unless you want to pay yourself, you'll do as I tell you."

> Son: "Look, I chose to come home over spring break to spend some time with you and go fishing like you said. But you know what? Sam said I could go camping with him and his family, so I'm outta here. Sorry I ever came." (Son picks up unpacked bags and slams the door on his way out)

PREPARING THE HEART

This second conversation is a peaceful dialogue between a father and his son. The details remain the same, but the Holy Spirit has prepared the heart and mind of the father to respond to his son in a more Christlike way—with *gentle instruction*. The difference in the father is that he has regularly asked the Holy Spirit to help him love his child as his heavenly Father loves His children.

To prepare the parent's heart before talking with his son, the Holy Spirit *gently* brings the following Scripture to the mind of the parent:

> Fathers, do not provoke your children, lest they become discouraged. (Colossians 3:21, NKJV)

> Fathers, do not provoke your children to anger, but bring them up in the discipline and instruction of the Lord. (Ephesians 6:4, NASB)

> Always be humble and gentle. Be patient with each other, making allowance for each other's faults because of your love. (Ephesians 4:2, NLT)

The *gentle* whisper of the Holy Spirit may have uttered some convicting questions to the father, such as:

- Have there been times in your life when your heavenly Father made it clear to you that it wasn't His will for you to do something, but you did it anyway?

- Did God patiently bear with you, extending His grace by giving you time to repent and mature without withdrawing His love for you?

- How is God wanting to conform *you* to the likeness of His Son through this disagreement with your child?

The Holy Spirit concludes His *gentle* instruction to the parent with this four-part exhortation:

Practice forbearance; calmly seek to understand your child's needs and limitations; share truth; and reaffirm your love for him.

As you compare the following *God-honoring communication* with the preceding monologues, consider the father's attitude in each conversation. Knowing that the words we speak reveal our hearts, what did the *harsh words* reveal about the dad? As you read this second conversation, listen closely to learn what change has taken place in the father's heart as he *gently instructs* his son.

GENTLE INSTRUCTION

As his son's car pulls into the driveway, the father hurries to the door to greet him. Although he notices his son's tattoo, he gives him a hug.

Father: "Welcome home, son. Great to see you. How was your drive home? The coals are hot, and the steaks will be ready whenever you are."

Son: (Returning his father's hug) "Great! I'm starving. Let me dump this stuff, and I'll be right out."

After listening to his son share about his classes and

friends at college over dinner, the conversation resumes:

Father: "Ready for some strawberry shortcake?"

Son: "Yeah, that sounds awesome."

Father: "I see that you decided to get a tattoo after all. Did it hurt?"

Son: "It did hurt, Dad. I know you tried to talk me out of getting a tattoo, but my buddies and I just thought it would be kinda fun if we all got one."

Father: "Although I don't approve of the tattoo, I want you to know that there's nothing you could do that would ever cause me to stop loving you."

Son: "Thanks, Dad. I love you too."

Father: "May I share something with you?"

Son: "Sure, Dad."

Father: "I realize you are at an age where your decisions should be between you and God, but you asked for my advice. And it really hurt me when you ignored my counsel."

Son: "I didn't mean to hurt you, Dad. I didn't think I ignored you. I remember you tried to discourage me, but you never told me *not* to get the tattoo. I figured it was my choice. I'm eighteen now."

Father: "That's true son; and that's my fault. I should have taken more time initially to ask why you wanted the tattoo, and to listen more closely to your response. I was wrong for not praying with you about it."

Son: "Dad, it's my fault, too. I probably wasn't listening to you because I really wanted the tattoo. I know you've taught me to pray first about all decisions, and to wait patiently for God's answers, but I didn't want to wait."

Father: "Son, I hope you know that my desire is not to keep you from doing things that you enjoy, but rather to encourage you to be careful to not engage in any behavior that Scripture instructs us to avoid."

Son: "In our telephone conversation, you did mention that as a Christian my body is a temple of the Holy Spirit. I didn't give it much thought at the time, but I think I get it now. I guess I figured my body was my body. I see now that I just wanted my own way. I'm sorry if my actions have hurt you, and if they have hurt God. I will pray and ask God to forgive me. Will you forgive me? I do respect you, Dad."

Father: "Son, I do forgive you. The tattoo isn't the issue. What's of concern, is your heart and your character. And you just proved to God and me that both your heart and character are just fine. I'm blessed to have you for a son. And I'm sorry if

I have hurt God and hurt you by my inaction or insufficient counsel. Will you forgive me? Would you like to pray together?"

Son: "Yes, I would like to pray with you, Dad."

In what ways is this second conversation more pleasing and honoring to God than the first? How did this transformation in communication happen for this father and son? What have you learned about the difference between ruling a child versus communicating with him or her?

May these father/son conversations serve to remind us that harsh words facilitate two monologues at best. Gentle instruction, on the other hand, smoothes the way for the building of close relationships.

How do *you* typically communicate with people who are under your authority when they do not meet your expectations – with harsh words, or gentle instruction? What do the words you speak reveal about *your* heart?

Blessed are the gentle, for they shall inherit the earth. (Matthew 5:5, NASB)

CHAPTER TWELVE

Above All Else, Continue in Love

If anyone says, "I love God," yet hates his brother, he is a liar. For anyone who does not love his brother, whom he has seen, cannot love God, whom he has not seen. And he has given us this command: Whoever loves God must also love his brother.

—1 John 4:19-21

Think of the church at large. What divisions! Think of the different bodies. Take the question of holiness, take the question of the cleansing blood, take the question of the baptism of the Spirit—what differences are caused among dear believers by such questions! That there are differences of opinion does not trouble me. We do not have the same constitution and temperament and mind. But how often hate, bitterness, contempt, separation, and unlovingness are caused by the holiest truths of God's Word! Our doctrines, our creeds, have been more important than love. We often think we are valiant for the truth, and we forget God's command to speak the truth *in love.* And it was so in the time of the Reformation between the Lutheran and Calvinistic churches. What bitterness there was in regard to communion, which was meant to be the bond of union among all believers! And so, through the ages, the very dearest truths of God have become mountains that have separated us.

If we want to pray in power, and if we want to expect the Holy Spirit to come down in power, and if we indeed want God to pour out His Spirit, we must enter into a covenant with God that we will love one another with a heavenly love.

—Andrew Murray, *Absolute Surrender*, pp. 35-36

TESTING THE SINCERITY OF OUR LOVE

Week after week, year after year, God has observed His people entering church buildings all across the world. He's watched, as we've sat down next to each other—seemingly comfortable—listening to worship music together—and appearing cordial with some degree of love for one another.

But God isn't so interested in us being comfortable. He is much more concerned about Christians being conformed to the likeness of His Son. So out of concern for the spiritual maturity of His children, our heavenly Father decided to test the *sincerity of our love for one another*. One means God has used to administer this test has been to allow conflict over **contemporary and traditional music** to surface in congregations all across America. Our response to this issue has indeed measured the sincerity of our love for one another. And while some have passed the test, others have failed.

IS OUR LOVE CONDITIONAL, OR UNCONDITIONAL?

To love conditionally means that we give our love when doing so serves our self-interests, and we withdraw our love when it doesn't.

Christ's love for us is the undeserved love of our Father for His children. It flows to us without conditions. That is the model that we have; to display a divinely inspired love even for those who disagree with us. Some people are more difficult than others to love, even to like, but we are called to present God's divine, unconditional love for one another despite our differences.

The following conversations display a difference between conditional love and unconditional love. The first conversation provides an example of withdrawing one's love when personal interests are not met. The second conversation shows how we can persevere in our love for one another, even though we disagree.

The setting of our conversation takes place in an older congregation with a rich history of evangelism and service to the community. A new worship leader has chosen to combine contemporary praise choruses with the usual diet of hymns. This has gotten more than a few members talking. One long-time member, Dave, decides to share his concerns with the worship leader, Ashley, after church.

FIRST CONVERSATION – TWO MONOLOGUES

Dave: "Do you have a minute, Ashley? I'd like to talk to you about the new songs you've been introducing."

Ashley: "Yeah, okay."

Dave: "It's about this new contemporary music you've been using. Have you really thought about it? I mean, I don't get anything out of it, and I know I'm not alone in that. It's too loud and sounds like a secular rock band. It causes people to focus so much on the beat of the music that it becomes entertainment, distracting them from truly worshipping God. Traditional hymns, now they convey deep reverence for God, and draw less attention to the music. And another thing..."

As Dave is talking, Ashley's thinking to herself that traditional music lacks passion and excitement for God. She's reminded of "holier than thous" who like to hear the nice words, but never put them into practice.

> **Ashley:** "Hymns don't seem to resonate well with the younger generation. I'm sorry you don't like contemporary music, but it is the style of worship my generation prefers. We believe it gives us more freedom to loosen up and freely express our praise and adoration for God."

Noticeably upset, Dave walks away.

The next morning Dave calls the church office and makes an appointment to meet with his pastor. Pastor Bill, quite aware of the stagnation of the congregation for the past several years, supports the worship leader and cites the need for their congregation to grow.

Dave and his wife are now quite perturbed, and begin to gossip about their pastor and worship leader with other members. Each Sunday, the more they hear the loud music and observe the gyrations of those singing and playing instruments, the more resentment they feel.

As the gossip spreads and the resentment grows into bitterness, they finally withdraw their love for Pastor Bill and Ashley, and leave the congregation. But not before their behavior has negatively influenced others.

TWO LIES THAT LURE US INTO WITHDRAWING LOVE
How does it happen that God's people withdraw our love for

one another over matters such as contemporary and traditional music, when God's desire is for us to be known by our love for one another?

It happens when Satan deceives us into believing two lies that lead to the withdrawing of our love for others.

Those **two lies** are:

1. **Issues** are more important to God than **relationships**. But they are not.

2. **Being "right"** is more important to God than **doing right**. But it is not.

There is a strong desire within human beings to be "right" and to get our way. So when someone comes along who doesn't see things exactly as we do, with the potential to keep us from getting our way, our sinful hearts and spiritual immaturity are often revealed.

In regard to contemporary and traditional music, Satan will try to exploit that weakness and immaturity by trying to deceive us into believing that the type of music we listen to is more important than maintaining our love for one another.

So be on guard against feelings of anger, resentment, or ill-will toward another person. Those feelings should be a red flag that signal a warning, alerting us to the fact that we are at risk of being deceived and of withdrawing our love for that person. May we encourage one another to not allow issues of concern to take precedent over our obedience to Christ's command that we love one another as He has loved us (John 13:34).

LOVE DOES NOT DEMAND ITS OWN WAY

In his letter to the church at Corinth, Paul writes to instruct the

Corinthians on genuine, godly love so they can practice loving one another in ways that will be pleasing to God. In the thirteenth chapter of 1 Corinthians, verses one through three, Paul wrote, "If I speak in the tongues of men and of angels, but have not love, I am only a resounding gong or a clanging cymbal. If I have the gift of prophecy and can fathom all mysteries and all knowledge, and if I have a faith that can move mountains, but have not love, I am nothing. If I give all I possess to the poor and surrender my body to the flames, but have not love, I gain nothing."

In verse five of chapter thirteen in the New Living Translation, Paul adds that "[Love] does not demand its own way."

Writing from prison several years later, Paul shares the following godly words of wisdom to the Colossians, "Bear with each other and forgive whatever grievances you may have against one another" (Colossians 3:13).

With those Scriptures in mind, let's look at how the conversation between Dave and Ashley can be honoring to God, *preserving their love for one another* in spite of their differences.

Before this conversation has begun, Dave has been challenged with the following questions:

1. Is being "right" about the issue and getting your way more important than your relationship and love for your sister in Christ?

2. Would your desire to obey God provide incentive for you to listen to some kinds of music you don't care for in order to maintain your love for Ashley?

As a result of Dave's wrestling with the Holy Spirit over this matter, Dave invites Ashley to have dinner with him and his wife. That evening, Ashley explains how she uses contemporary music to reach the next generation with the gospel.

SECOND CONVERSATION – DIALOGUE

Ashley: "This church has always been concerned about reaching out to the unsaved. But most hymns were written generations ago and don't sound anything like the music that most unsaved people listen to these days. So if an unbeliever comes to our service and hears only the old hymns, the experience is going to seem really alien to them. They wouldn't connect with worship at all. If we are serious about evangelism, we've got to make our service welcoming for people who are seeking to learn more about Jesus."

Dave: "I never thought of it that way. I admit that I've probably been opposed to the contemporary music mainly because I, personally, am more comfortable with hymns. Ashley, I appreciate your sensitivity to evangelism."

Ashley: "And I appreciate your candor and flexibility, Dave."

As Dave and Ashley continue to talk, they agree to keep monitoring the balance of music. Neither wants to offend those who are blessed by hymns, and each wants to provide music that the younger generation can better relate to, with lyrics honoring to God. Both further agree to listen to both styles of music with an open mind, being other-minded and

CHAPTER THIRTEEN

—

Jesus' Forceful Response to the Money Changers

*On reaching Jerusalem, Jesus entered the temple area and
began driving out those who were buying and selling there.
He overturned the tables of the money changers and the
benches of those selling doves, and would not allow anyone
to carry merchandise through the temple courts. And as he
taught them, he said, "Is it not written: " 'My house will
be called a house of prayer for all nations'? But you have
made it 'a den of robbers.' "*

*The chief priests and the teachers of the law heard this
and began looking for a way to kill him, for they feared him,
because the whole crowd was amazed at his teaching.*

—Mark 11:15-18

When the holiness of God and His worship was at stake,
Jesus took fast and furious action. Yet, although His
physical action was forceful, it was not cruel. The moderation
of His actions is seen in the fact that no riotous uproar
occurred.

—John MacArthur, *The MacArthur Study Bible*, p. 1579

The Court of the Gentiles was that part of the temple they were permitted to use for prayer and worship of God. Worshippers came from all over Israel and the Roman Empire to Jerusalem. Opportunistic merchants set up areas in the outer courts, such as the Court of the Gentiles, so that travelers could purchase animals there to present as temple sacrifices. This was easier than bringing their animals with them on their journey. It also helped to eliminate the risk of animals not passing the High Priest's required inspection. What the traveler may have mistaken as a convenience, the money changers used as an opportunity for their own financial gain. Since the traveler may have only carried Greek or Roman money, they were easy prey for those who offered an exchange to the required temple tax in Jewish or Tyrian coinage.

JESUS THE TEACHER, IN THE MIDST OF CONFLICT
The Apostle John wrote an account of Jesus cleansing the temple toward the beginning of His ministry (John 2:13-16). The synoptic gospels tell of Jesus cleansing the temple a second time at the end of His ministry (Matthew 21:12-13; Mark 11:15-18; Luke 19:45-46). The second cleansing took place because the Jewish nation still hadn't understood the *authority* of Jesus.

These written accounts reveal that the animal merchants and money changers were exploiting the sacrificial practices of the Jews for monetary gain. Such practices disrupted worship, and showed great irreverence for a holy God.

To end these activities at the beginning of Jesus' ministry, He drove the traders from the temple with the command, "Do not make My Father's house a house of merchandise!" (John 2:16, NKJV). As He drove them out toward the end of His ministry, Jesus asked the question, "Is it not written: " 'My house will be called a house of prayer for all nations'? But you have made it 'a den of robbers' " (Mark 11:17).

In Mark 11:18, it's important to note what caused the amazement of the crowd who watched and heard Jesus as He cleansed the temple. Was it His forceful response? No. What astonished them was *His teaching*. Even while administering a forceful response in the midst of conflict, Jesus' supernatural ability to teach spiritual truth was never diminished.

By His words and actions, Jesus communicated at least six significant truths to the crowd who watched and listened with amazement. First, He taught of His Deity as He referred to God as His Father. Second, Jesus gave them opportunity to understand the need for an intimate, loyal relationship to God, as they heard Jesus intervene in behalf of His Father, revealing a oneness with Him. Third, He testified to the holiness of God. Fourth, He taught the crowd that there was a need for separating what is intended for spiritual purposes from that which is worldly. A sacred house of prayer was to be set apart from greedy robbers, who were eager to exploit others for financial gain. Fifth, Jesus taught the Jews to be respectful of the Gentiles who had come to the temple to pray and worship God, as Jesus had come to save people of all nations. Sixth, Jesus made it clear that He was a person with the *authority* to take any action He deemed necessary.

ARE CHRISTIANS TO RESPOND AS JESUS DID?

For the past seventeen years I've been teaching biblical principles to help prepare God's people to respond as Christ would to people with opposing views. During almost every seminar I've presented, someone in the audience invariably asks the question, "What about the money changers?"

In response to that question, I present the following for *you*, the reader of this book, to prayerfully consider during a quiet time with God.

1. Can you think of any Scripture in which Christians are commanded or instructed to respond to conflict in the way Jesus responded to the money changers?

2. As you read the following commands from Jesus, what do you discern to be His will in regard to how we are to respond to people with opposing views?

> But I tell you: Love your enemies and pray for those who persecute you. (Matthew 5:44)

> Do to others what you would have them do to you. (Matthew 7:12)

> Love your neighbor as yourself. (Matthew 22:39)

> As I have loved you, so you must love one another. (John 13:34)

LOVE INCLUDES TRUTH AND ACCOUNTABILITY

Although this book is about communicating the love of Christ to others, it's not a message of grace without truth and accountability, because that is not the message of the Bible. God's Word teaches us to correct, rebuke, and encourage one another, but the question is, how are we to love one another in those ways?

Paul provides some insight. He explains that we are to do so "with great patience and careful instruction" (2 Timothy 4:2). He offers additional wise counsel with the words, "Dear brothers and sisters, if another believer is overcome by some sin, you who are godly should gently and humbly help that person back onto the right path. And be careful not to fall into the same temptation yourself" (Galatians 6:1, NLT).

If *church discipline* is in order, the Word of God provides clear steps on how to administer such discipline:

1. If your brother sins against you, go and show him his fault, just between the two of you. If he listens to you, you have won your brother over. (Matthew 18:15)

    > Such loving discipline provides great opportunity for two Christians to practice *Christlike civility* by communicating through dialogue in the Spirit of Christ.

2. But if he will not listen, take one or two others along, so that 'every matter may be established by the testimony of two or three witnesses.' (Matthew 18:16)

    > This second step provides yet another opportunity for *Christlike dialogue* among a small group of fellow Christians. They should respectfully remind each other that their purpose for convening is to assist in sorting out what is truth in order to establish the facts, *without showing favoritism* toward anyone in the process (1 Timothy 5:21).

3. If he refuses to listen to them, tell it to the church… (Matthew 18:17)

    > The reason for sharing with the entire congregation is so that as a church family they can be praying for the repentance and restoration of the straying member of their family.

4. ...and if he refuses to listen even to the church, treat him as you would a pagan or a tax collector. (Matthew 18:17)

> How are we to treat pagans? With the love of Christ, as He has treated us.

> *The Message* explains it this way, "If he won't listen to the church, you'll have to start over from scratch, confront him with the need for repentance, and offer again God's forgiving love" (Matthew 18:17, MSG).

GIVING HIGHEST PRIORITY TO CHURCH DISCIPLINE

Sadly, because of the busyness of life, church discipline often becomes just one more item on the agenda of an elders' meeting. When it comes up, it's often addressed briefly in a way that says, "If the accused repents, we love him and he can remain as a member of our congregation. But if he refuses to repent, he's out of here, and we don't care if he ever comes back." *Then he is forgotten.*

How sad and tragic it is when church leaders do not give the reconciliation and restoration of a straying brother or sister in Christ their highest priority. For when we fail to have the kind of Christlike love that makes time to pursue sinners, especially one who is a member of the family, we fail to love them as Jesus has loved us.

NOT FORGETTING THOSE WHO STRAY

The goal of church discipline is to see a brother or sister repent of sin and be restored to fellowship with God and the body of believers.

Even if there is no repentance on the part of the person

who is being disciplined, and that person is told to leave the fellowship, he should not be written off and forgotten. Instead, members should continue in prayer for him. The pastor or other members of the church should take time to write, call, or go see the one who has gone astray, with the goal of restoring him back to fellowship (Matthew 18:10-14). In that way, he can have the opportunity to experience the love of a heavenly Father who pursues His children.

IS TOLERANCE LOVING?

Is tolerance an act of love? Or does it rather convey apathy, indifference and irresponsibility by failing to warn and discourage people from participating in behavior that can hurt them and others? It most likely depends on how one defines tolerance.

The world's definition of tolerance and the biblical definition of tolerance are quite different. The tolerance message of our world today not only teaches people to tolerate both sin and sinner, but to also *show respect for and even promote the practices and behaviors of others*, even if those behaviors are displeasing to God, harmful to those who practice them, and detrimental to society. Christians must not be deceived into believing this lie, for to accept that lie would be to reject the absolute truth of the Word of God, and to have a lack of love for the people who will be hurt, some eternally, if Christians don't care enough and are not courageous enough to *speak the truth in love* to people ignorant of what the Word of God teaches.

God not only tolerates sinners, He loves them. While Jesus was here on earth, He engaged all kinds of people in dialogue and conversations from prostitutes, thieves and tax collectors to military leaders and religious rulers. In fact, the reason Jesus came to earth was to suffer and die to save sinners, because of His great love for us. But He never implied that sinful behavior was acceptable. As Jesus spoke with the woman caught in the act of adultery, He didn't condemn the woman, but He did tell her, "Go now and leave your life of sin" (John 8:11). And as Christians, we are to follow Christ's example of loving sinners in spite of our sin, yet never condoning it.

While God loves sinners like you and me, He hates the wickedness and evil of sin. And it is God's will for His people to hate sin as well, as we can learn from the following passages of Scripture.

> Your throne, O God, will last for ever and ever; a scepter of justice will be the scepter of your king-dom. You love righteousness and hate wicked-ness... (Psalm 45:6-7)

> Your eyes are too pure to look on evil; you cannot tolerate wrong. (Habakkuk 1:13a)

> Let those who love the Lord hate evil... (Psalm 97:10)

> Love must be sincere. Hate what is evil; cling to what is good. (Romans 12:9)

BEWARE OF IGNORING OR TOLERATING WILLFUL SIN

It's important for church leadership to give high priority to administering church discipline in loving ways, and to not be deceived into tolerating and ignoring the *willful sin* of any member of their congregation.

In 1 Corinthians 5:1-13, we hear of such exhortation from Paul. As believers in Corinth had conformed to the world around them, their carnality had taken a devastating toll on

122

their spiritual life. So much so, that Paul had to call for the immediate removal of a sexually immoral person within their congregation. Apparently, the leadership of that church had failed to administer church discipline, in spite of the sin being an extraordinarily grievous one.

Paul was keenly aware that such evil could put that body of believers at great risk. He understood that sin, when *tolerated*, could spread and defile an entire congregation. To prevent the harmful influence of an unrepentant church member, Paul made it clear that this person needed to leave the congregation.

As a wise and godly man, Paul explained to the church leadership that his concern regarding church discipline had to do with Christians, not immoral pagans. People who are not Christians are for God to judge. But Paul made it clear that Christians should not associate with a professing Christian who *willfully* returns to the immoral and sinful practices of a pagan society.

Nevertheless, Paul still desired the salvation and restoration of this individual by saying, "Then you must throw this man out and hand him over to Satan so that his sinful nature will be destroyed and he himself will be saved on the day the Lord returns" (1 Corinthians 5:5, NLT).

One might wonder, "How is turning someone over to Satan and not associating with them a loving thing to do?"

First, one of Satan's long time strategies has been to deceive people into believing that evil is good. When people have been deceived in this way, some may never come to the realization that what they are doing is wrong, unless and until they experience the painful consequences of their sin. When someone hits bottom after suffering the pain that accompanies the discipline of a loving heavenly Father, there is a greater likelihood that person will look up and see their need for God.

Oftentimes it is in these darkest of hours that we experience intimacy with God, an awakening to the awfulness of sin, and an awareness of how much it grieves the heart of a loving God, all in ways that bring one to repentance.

Second, to "not associate" does not mean to abandon. It does mean that we should not condone sinful behavior, nor join in such activity. But we can seek to love and serve in ways that meet needs. We can also be prepared to teach with great patience and careful instruction, when there is opportunity to do so.

For example, participating in a rally to promote the behavior of practicing homosexuals would not be a loving thing to do. Nor is it loving to counsel someone to get a divorce because you have sympathy for one spouse, when there are no scriptural grounds to justify a divorce. Why? Because God makes it clear that while His love remains for people who practice homosexuality, and although He doesn't withdraw His love from people who have been divorced, He still hates both divorce (Malach 2:16) and homosexuality (Leviticus 20:13).

On the other hand, serving at a hospice to care for, listen to and pray with a homosexual who is dying of AIDS is a very loving thing to do, as is teaching and offering encouragement at a divorce recovery workshop.

Although Jesus didn't *tolerate* the behavior of the money changers, I'm sure He would not have driven any of them away if they returned later to the temple for prayer and to worship God.

INFLUENCING THE WORLD, RATHER THAN BECOMING WORLDLY

In his letter to Roman Christians Paul warned them, "Do not conform any longer to the pattern of this world, but be transformed by the renewing of your mind" (Romans 12:2a). We as Christians of today will be wise to heed Paul's admonishment, for there are many ways in which Christians have ignored the spiritual, and conformed to what is worldly.

Embracing the world's definition of tolerance is one such example. Forsaking what the Bible teaches about hating evil, many Christians have allowed the world to deceive them into believing that it is unloving and judgmental of anyone who is not accepting of the sinful behavior of others, even though it is unacceptable to God and harmful to society. When Christians complacently embrace that lie, they have become worldly, rather than influencing the world for Christ.

Christians also conform to this world when we are unloving toward people with whom we experience conflict. If two Christians are unwilling to maintain their love for one another while discussing their differences, how is that any different from how an unsaved worldly person would respond? What if the disagreement is with an unbeliever? Will the Christian consider the possibility that the opposing party has never personally experienced the grace, forgiveness, acceptance and affirmation of God, and that they may be talking with a person who has never had even one relative or friend ever pray for them? Will the Christian be mindful of the fact that the non-Christian is still deceived, hasn't come to a knowledge of the truth, and doesn't understand how much their sinful behavior grieves their loving Creator?

If the Christian responds with truth, but without love and compassion, that Christian has forgotten he has been forgiven (2 Peter 1:3-9), and has failed to remember the grace and mercy God has extended to him.

Jesus had compassion for sinners without condoning our sin. His desire was and is for the salvation of sinners. Is that your desire? Do you have compassion for the non-Christian who doesn't see things exactly as you do? Do you pray for their salvation? Do you seek to speak the truth in love and gently instruct them so that God might grant them repentance and lead them to a knowledge of His truth? Have you ever had such a sharp disagreement with a brother or sister in Christ, that you withdrew your love for them? Based upon your answers to those questions, would you say that you are more likely to influence the world for Christ, or that you are being conformed to this world?

A MEMORABLE MEETING

Many years ago, I served as the program director for a prison ministry in Colorado. I interviewed prison inmates. I also interviewed Christians who were interested in building a friendship with a prison inmate. I would then match them up and introduce them to each other so they could begin building a relationship with mutual respect for one another.

One day as I was interviewing an inmate, he began to share his story. He started by telling me that he was a homosexual, and dying from AIDS. He went on to say that his father had been both a doctor and a lawyer, who frequently abused him. The abuse became so severe that at the age of twelve social services placed the boy with foster care parents, a couple who claimed to be Christians.

Later, as this young boy began to experience some homosexual tendencies, the foster parents learned about it and kicked him out of their home. Rejected by his dad, taken away from his parents, and rejected by those he knew to be Christians, he explained that he was left alone to fend for himself. Then he shared these words with me, "Here I am in my thirties, a practicing homosexual who is in prison, dying from AIDS, but I want you to know, that even though I have been rejected before, I'm willing to let you match me up with a

Christian as long as they don't come here and tell me how bad and wrong I am, and that I need to change."

This prisoner was in need of forgiveness and the loving-kindness of Jesus Christ, not a lecture from someone else telling him how bad and wrong he was.

BE VERY CAREFUL HOW YOU RESPOND

Getting back to the money changers, Jesus' response does not give Christians the green light to fight or to correct anyone *harshly* who the Christian perceives is doing something offensive to God.

Remember that Jesus had the *authority* to take any action He deemed appropriate with the money changers. He knew exactly what to say and do when responding to them because He was one with His heavenly Father, and knew the will of God in all situations. How about *you*? Do you have the *authority* as Jesus did, to tell others what they need to do? Will you be walking so closely with Jesus Christ that you will know exactly how *Jesus wants to respond through you* during the next disagreement you have with someone?

Keep praying, and don't dismiss the fact that Jesus loves sinners, but hates sin.

CHAPTER FOURTEEN

Jesus' Judgmental Words to the Pharisees

Then Jesus said to the crowds and to his disciples: "The teachers of the law and the Pharisees sit in Moses' seat. So you must obey them and do everything they tell you. But do not do what they do, for they do not practice what they preach."

—Matthew 23:1-3

With tens of thousands of divorces, lawsuits, and church splits pitting Christian against Christian each year, "death by friendly fire" has become a crisis issue for all believers. Have you heard what factor is most often cited by those leaving the church? It's hypocrisy in the church— Christians *preaching* peace and *talking* peace, but often not *living* peace in their relationships.

—Ken Sande, President of Peacemaker Ministries

THEY KNEW NOTHING OF GOD'S LOVE

Jesus rebuked the Pharisees and teachers of the law because they rejected Him. As Jesus cleared the temple and taught the people through Scripture, the chief priests and the teachers of the law heard Jesus and "began looking for a way to kill him" (Mark 11:18). Their willful choice to reject the Savior prevented them from receiving the gift of the Holy Spirit. And without the Holy Spirit, they had no power to love others with the love of Christ—no power to practice what they preached.

Jesus condemned their efforts at establishing a righteousness of their own. They were not willing to give God the glory for the righteousness that comes to those who have faith in Jesus Christ (2 Corinthians 5:21). Because of their blatant rejection of Jesus, He made the truth of their hypocrisy known with bold statements such as:

> Woe to you, teachers of the law and Pharisees, you hypocrites! You shut the kingdom of heaven in men's faces. You yourselves do not enter, nor will you let those enter who are trying to. (Matthew 23:13-14)

> ...You give a tenth of your spices—mint, dill and cumin. But you have neglected the more important matters of the law—justice, mercy and faithfulness. You should have practiced the latter, without neglecting the former. You blind guides! You strain out a gnat but swallow a camel. (Matthew 23:23-24)

GOD KNOWS HEARTS, BUT WE DON'T

While our heavenly Father is a forgiving and compassionate God, He's also a God of justice who hates sin. And because He knows the hearts of all people (1 Kings 8:39), and understands every motive behind their thoughts (1 Chronicles 28:9), He is correct in His judgment every time.

But didn't Jesus usually extend grace, mercy and compassion to sinners? Why such judgmental words to those Pharisees? I believe the following words from Jesus to the religious leaders shed clear light as to why.

> ...Jesus said to them, "I tell you the truth, the tax collectors and the prostitutes are entering the kingdom of God ahead of you. For John came to you to show you the way of righteousness, and you did not believe him, but the tax collectors and the prostitutes did. And even after you saw this, you did not repent and believe him. (Matthew 21:31-32)

> O Jerusalem, Jerusalem, you who kill the prophets and stone those sent to you, how often I have longed to gather your children together, as a hen gathers her chicks under her wings, but you were not willing. (Matthew 23:37)

On many prior occasions, Jesus had offered grace, mercy and compassion to those leaders. During numerous conversations, He offered Himself to them. Each time, they failed to acknowledge that He was the Messiah promised to them, and willfully chose to reject Jesus as their Savior and Lord, along with His divine authority.

So Jesus, knowing their hearts and being the Judge (John 5:22), had every right to speak truthful words of judgment, and to condemn the self-righteous hypocrisy of certain teachers of the law and Pharisees. But to His followers, Jesus teaches us not to pass judgment on others (Romans 2:1). Why? Because *we don't know people's hearts, and we are not God.*

And just as Jesus despised the self-righteous attitude of the religious hypocrites when He was here on earth, He continues to condemn the self-righteous attitude of today's Christians who forget they are forgiven and fail to extend the *unmerited love* they have received from God to others.

Do you ever perceive yourself to be more spiritually mature than others? If so, do you use that maturity to love, serve, and disciple others for God's glory, or do you look down on people you perceive to be less mature than yourself with a critical, judgmental, "holier-than-thou" spirit?

If any self-righteousness remains in our hearts, may the God of grace grant us repentance as we solemnly and prayerfully consider Christ's warning in Matthew 5:20: "Unless your righteousness surpasses that of the Pharisees and the teachers of the law, you will certainly not enter the kingdom of heaven."

As we remember the *amazing grace* God has extended to us, may God use the following words to bring conviction that leads to repentance of any spiritual pride that is within our hearts.

Beware Of Criticizing Others

"Judge not, that you be not judged" (Matthew 7:1, NKJV).

Jesus' instructions in regard to judging others is very simply put; He says, *"Don't."* The average Christian is the most piercingly critical individual known.... The Holy Spirit is the only one in the proper position to criticize, and He alone is

---

able to show what is wrong without hurting and wounding. It is impossible to enter into fellowship with God when you are in a critical mood. Criticism serves to make you harsh, vindictive, and cruel, and leaves you with the soothing and flattering idea that you are somehow superior to others...You must constantly beware of anything that causes you to think of yourself as a superior person.

—Oswald Chambers,
My Utmost for His Highest, June 17

CHAPTER FIFTEEN

———

Paul Argued Boldly,
But What Did He Argue About?

Paul entered the synagogue and spoke boldly there for three months, arguing persuasively about the kingdom of God.

—Acts 19:8

A biding in Him [Jesus Christ], you receive from Him *His Spirit of love and compassion toward sinners*, which makes you want to see them blessed. By nature the heart is full of selfishness. Even in the believer, his own salvation and happiness is too often his only object. But abiding in Jesus, you come into contact with His infinite love, and its fire begins to burn within your heart; you see the beauty of love; you learn to look upon loving, serving, and saving your fellowmen as the highest privilege a disciple of Jesus can have. Abiding in Christ, your heart learns to feel the wretched condition of sinners still in darkness, and what dishonor is done to God by their alienation from Him. With Christ you begin to bear the burden of souls, the burden of sins not your own. As you are more closely united to Him, some measure of that passion for souls that urged Him to Calvary begins to breathe within you, and you are ready to follow His footsteps, to forsake the heaven of your own happiness and devote your life to win the souls Christ has taught you to love. The very spirit of the Vine is love, and this spirit of love streams into the branch that

135

abides in Him.

—Andrew Murray, *Abiding in Christ*, pp. 122-123

LEARNING TO THINK SPIRITUALLY

As Jesus explained to His disciples that He must suffer, be killed, and on the third day be raised to life, Peter took Jesus aside and rebuked Him, saying, "God forbid it, Lord! This shall never happen to You." To which Jesus replied, "Get behind Me, Satan! You are a stumbling block to Me; for you are not setting your mind on God's interests, but man's" (Matthew 16:21-23, NASB).

Peter's rebuke of Jesus revealed that his mind was set on the *worldly* interests of men; such as recognition, political power, and military might. Whereas the *spiritual* interests of God include love for people, the salvation of souls, and the transformation of lives.

Peter later came to understand the difference and would go on to boldly proclaim the gospel while humbly feeding and shepherding the lambs and sheep of God.

Some time later Paul too would get the message, and begin to *think spiritually*. After a unique encounter with Jesus on the road to Damascus and his miraculous conversion, Paul would spend the remainder of his life pointing people to Jesus Christ.

Listen to how Paul's words reveal a mind focused on the spiritual interests of God, rather than the worldly interests of men. His focus is on Jesus Christ, rather then the social or political concerns of those times.

In Antioch

Paul said, "I want you to know that through Jesus the forgiveness of sins is proclaimed to you. Through

him everyone who believes is justified from everything you could not be justified from by the law of
Moses." (Acts 13:38-39)

<u>At Mars Hill in Athens</u>
Paul went into the synagogue, and reasoned with
the Jews from the Scriptures, explaining and proving
that the Christ had to suffer and rise from the dead.
He said, "This Jesus I am proclaiming to you is the
Christ." (Acts 17:2-3)

<u>To the elders of the Ephesus church</u>
Paul said, "I consider my life worth nothing to me,
if only I may finish the race and complete the task
the Lord Jesus has given me—the task of testifying
to the gospel of God's grace." (Acts 20:24)

<u>In Rome</u>
From morning till evening he explained and
declared to them the kingdom of God and tried to
convince them about Jesus from the Law of Moses
and from the Prophets. Boldly and without hindrance he preached the kingdom of God and taught
about the Lord Jesus Christ. (Acts 28:23, 31)

Paul reasoned with people from the Scriptures—explaining and proving—testifying and declaring—teaching, preaching and trying to convince others that Jesus is the Christ, the
Savior of the world. He boldly proclaimed that anyone who
chose to believe in the Lord Jesus Christ would have their sins
forgiven and be reconciled to God.
Why did Paul focus on Jesus Christ and salvation, rather
than devoting time and energy to addressing social and

political issues? Because Paul understood that Jesus Christ is the answer to *all* of life's challenges.

SHARING THE ANSWER TO LIFE'S CHALLENGES

Who embodies true love and respect to make a lasting marriage? **Jesus Christ**

Who sets people free from anxiety and depression? **Jesus Christ**

Who can transform lives so people can experience love, joy, and peace? **Jesus Christ**

Who releases those held captive to poverty and oppression? **Jesus Christ**

Who is a friend to widows and orphans in their times of loneliness and need? **Jesus Christ**

Who is the only hope for peace in this world? **Jesus Christ**

Who alone must one believe in for the salvation of our souls, the forgiveness of our sins, and to receive God's promise of eternal life? **Jesus Christ**

Who is the answer to all of life's challenges? **Jesus Christ**

What people believe about Jesus Christ will determine where we spend eternity.

What priority we give to His interests—to setting our hearts on what He wants—will determine whether we have any real purpose and significance while living here on earth.

How much we love this Person—how much we trust

Him—how often we obey Him will determine whether or not we reflect His likeness and respond as He would to conflict, adversity, trials and tribulations.

The extent to which Christ's disciples remain in Him and truly become known by our love for one another will determine the degree to which life's challenges will truly be solved.

Rather than look to man for answers to life's challenges, why not simply share the answer: **JESUS CHRIST**.

That's what Paul did.

Are Christians of today *boldly* proclaiming Jesus Christ as the answer to life's challenges? Is that what *you* are doing? If not, why not? During your conversations with people of opposing views, do you deliberately point them to Jesus Christ? If no, why not?

WHAT IT MEANS TO STAND FIRM

Over the years, I've heard people make the comment, "We need to take a stand," usually in reference to a social, religious, or moral concern that is being addressed politically. In the following Scripture, Paul explains what *standing firm* meant to him.

> I consider everything a loss compared to the surpassing greatness of knowing Christ Jesus my Lord, for whose sake I have lost all things. I consider them rubbish, that I may gain Christ and be found in him, not having a righteousness of my own that comes from the law, but that which is through faith in Christ—the righteousness that comes from God and is by faith. I want to know Christ and the power of his resurrection and the fellowship of sharing in his sufferings, becoming like him in his death I press on toward the goal to

win the prize for which God has called me heavenward in Christ Jesus.

All of us who are mature should take such a view of things. And if on some point you think differently, that too God will make clear to you. Only let us live up to what we have already attained.

...Our citizenship is in heaven. And we eagerly await a Savior from there, the Lord Jesus Christ, who, by the power that enables him to bring everything under his control, will transform our lowly bodies so that they will be like his glorious body.

Therefore, my brothers, you whom I love and long for, my joy and crown, that is how you should stand firm in the Lord, dear friends! (Philippians 3:8-10, 14-16, 20-21; 4:1).

To Paul, *standing firm* meant:

- Giving up everything for the sake of knowing Jesus.
- Being found righteous through faith in Christ.
- Knowing the power of Jesus' resurrection.
- Experiencing the fellowship of sharing in Christ's sufferings.
- Becoming like Jesus in His death, by dying to self and living to please God.
- Moving toward the goal to win the prize of God's calling to become more like Christ.
- Living up to what he had already attained, by acting as a child of God should act.

When you talk with people who disagree with you, do your words and does your example give evidence that you are *"standing firm"* in the ways Paul would define those words?

Listen to Paul's words of exhortation:

> Be on your guard; stand firm in the faith; be men of courage; be strong. Do everything in love.
> (1 Corinthians 16:13-14)

If you have decided to "take a stand" for or against a particular issue or concern, in what ways do your actions and words indicate that *you* are doing everything in love?

How will you prepare to *courageously share Jesus with boldness*, as Paul did?

PART FIVE

Jesus Met Needs With Grace And Truth

CHAPTER SIXTEEN

The Need for Grace and Truth

For the law was given through Moses; grace and truth came through Jesus Christ.

—John 1:17

Truth without grace breeds a self-righteous legalism that poisons the church and pushes the world away from Christ.

Grace without truth breeds moral indifference and keeps people from seeing their need for Christ.

When we offend everybody, it's because we've taken on the truth mantle without grace. When we offend nobody, it's because we've watered down truth in the name of grace.

If we minimize grace, the world sees no hope for salvation. If we minimize truth, the world sees no need for salvation. To show the world Jesus, we must offer unabridged grace and truth, emphasizing both, apologizing for neither.

We need to examine ourselves and correct ourselves. We who are truth-oriented need to go out of our way to affirm grace. We who are grace-oriented need to go out of our way to affirm truth.

People thirst for the real Jesus. Nothing less can satisfy.

We show people Jesus only when we show them grace and truth.

—Randy Alcorn, *The Grace and Truth Paradox*, pp. 18, 20, 87-88, 92

ONLY ONE CERTAIN WAY

One day I was presenting a seminar on Christlike dialogue to a group of lawyers, when one attorney raised his hand and said, "This is great material, but how do we apply these principles in our law practice?"

I replied, "I know of only one certain way and that is to *abide in Christ*. Jesus said, "I am the vine; you are the branches. If a man remains in me and I in him, he will bear much fruit; apart from me you can do nothing" (John 15:5). Only by maintaining an intimate relationship with Jesus will you know how to respond in any given situation, and here's why. God may lead one of you to leave your law practice and become a full-time mediator and peacemaker. With another attorney, the Holy Spirit may want you to counsel your client to relinquish their rights and lose the case. Why? Because God knows that particular opponent is in need of *grace*; the unmerited love that will draw that person to Jesus Christ. God's wisdom for a third lawyer might be to move forward boldly and win the case for your client. Why the difference? Because in this case, God knows the opposing party is in need of *truth and accountability*, rather than grace and mercy."

How can *you* know if the person you are discussing differences with is in need of grace, or in need of truth, or if that person is in need of both grace and truth? Only by abiding in Christ, so that His Spirit enables you to discern the need and respond accordingly.

Practically speaking, what does it mean to "abide" or "remain in" Christ? The Bible answers that question for us. In 1 John 2:24, the apostle John wrote, "See that what you have heard from the beginning remains in you. If it does, you also will remain in the Son and in the Father." He goes on to clarify in 1 John 3:11, "This is the message you heard from the beginning: We should love one another."

AVOIDING FALSE GRACE AND HARSH TRUTH

Apart from Jesus Christ, most of us are at risk of erring in one of two ways: false grace or harsh truth. Harsh truth is usually spoken when the motive is to enforce compliance. False grace occurs when we deceive ourselves into believing that being silent or showing sympathy is the most loving action we can take. But that simply isn't true in situations where the opposing party is in need of loving rebuke or admonishment, especially when our real motive is to avoid the anxiety we typically experience with conflict.

In which way are *you* most at risk of erring when communicating with people who disagree with you—*false grace* or *harsh truth*?

So how do we extend grace without compromising truth? How does one communicate absolute truth *in love* to those who believe in relativism? How do we convey godly tolerance toward sinners, without condoning worldly tolerance of sin? And how can we know if someone with an opposing view is in need of grace and mercy, truth and accountability, or all four?

There's only one certain way: *abide in Christ*. Why? Because Christ knows every person's heart, and we don't. But if we abide in Christ, remain focused on His interests and His will, we can through the power of His Holy Spirit, discern a person's need.

MEETING NEEDS (My Job)
CHANGING MINDS (The Holy Spirit's Job)

If we want to respond with grace and truth as Christ would, meeting the needs of the person we are talking with must take priority over our effort to change their minds. As our focus is on communication and dialogue, we'll focus on emotional and spiritual needs, rather than physical needs.

147

Three *emotional* needs of people are listed below:

- To be loved
- To be accepted
- To be affirmed

Two *spiritual* needs of people are:

- To know Jesus Christ as Savior – *Salvation*
- To know Jesus Christ as Lord – *Sanctification*

In chapters 17 and 18, I share two of Jesus' life-changing dialogues. Each helps us to learn from our Lord's example, ways of communicating both grace and truth to meet a person's emotional and spiritual needs.

CHAPTER SEVENTEEN

Life-Changing Dialogue #1

Here is a trustworthy saying that deserves full acceptance:
Christ Jesus came into the world to save sinners.

—1 Timothy 1:15

My study of Jesus' life convinces me that whatever barriers we must overcome in treating "different" people cannot compare to what a holy God—who dwelled in the Most Holy Place...overcame when he descended to join us on planet Earth.

A prostitute, a wealthy exploiter, a demon-possessed woman, a Roman soldier, a Samaritan with running sores and another Samaritan with serial husbands—I marvel that Jesus gained the reputation as being a "friend of sinners" like these.

All of us in the church need "grace-healed eyes" to see the potential in others for the same grace that God has so lavishly bestowed on us.

—Philip Yancey, *What's So Amazing About Grace*, p. 175

DIALOGUE AT THE WELL (John 4:1-26)

As Jesus was passing through Samaria on His way to Galilee, He came to a town in Samaria called Sychar, near the plot of ground Jacob had given to his son Joseph. Jacob's well was there, and Jesus, tired from His journey, sat down by the well.

There was a kingdom purpose behind the timing of this stop, because it was at this well that Jesus would soon begin a *life-changing dialogue* with a Samaritan woman.

In Jesus' day, Jews didn't talk to Samaritans, men didn't talk to women in public, and religious people didn't talk to persons of questionable morals. Yet listen to the conversation between Jesus and a Samaritan woman who has come at noon to draw water.

> **Jesus:** "Will you give me a drink?"

> Samaritan Woman: "You are a Jew and I am a Samaritan woman. How can you ask me for a drink?"

> **Jesus:** "If you knew the gift of God and who it is that asks you for a drink, you would have asked him and he would have given you living water."

> Samaritan Woman: "Sir, you have nothing to draw with and the well is deep. Where can you get this living water? Are you greater than our father Jacob, who gave us the well and drank from it himself, as did also his sons and his flocks and herds?"

> **Jesus:** "Everyone who drinks this water will be thirsty again, but whoever drinks the water I give

him will never thirst. Indeed, the water I give will become in him a spring of water welling up to eternal life."

Samaritan Woman: "Sir, give me this water so that I won't get thirsty and have to keep coming here to draw water."

Jesus: "Go, call your husband and come back."

Samaritan Woman: "I have no husband."

Jesus: "You are right when you say you have no husband. The fact is, you have had five husbands, and the man you now have is not your husband. What you have just said is quite true."

Samaritan Woman: "Sir, I can see that you are a prophet. Our fathers worshiped on this mountain, but you Jews claim that the place where we must worship is in Jerusalem."

Jesus: "Believe me, woman, a time is coming when you will worship the Father neither on this mountain nor in Jerusalem. You Samaritans worship what you do not know; we worship what we do know, for salvation is from the Jews. Yet a time is coming and has now come when the true worshippers will worship the Father in spirit and truth, for they are the kind of worshipers the Father seeks. God is spirit, and his worshipers must worship in spirit and in truth."

> Samaritan Woman: "I know that Messiah" (called Christ) "is coming. When he comes, he will explain everything to us."

> **Jesus:** "I who speak to you am he."

MEETING AN OUTCAST'S NEEDS THROUGH GRACE AND TRUTH

Jesus didn't feel it was necessary to conform to the culture around Him, as others did. Though this woman was a Samaritan and an outcast in the Hebrew community, Jesus didn't hesitate to extend **grace to meet her emotional need for love, acceptance, and affirmation**. The affirmation of her worth as a person began with the fact that He, a Jewish man would sit down and talk with her, a Samaritan woman. Not only did Jesus talk openly with the woman in broad daylight for anyone to see, but He *listened* as she spoke. He *cared* about what she had to say.

The woman's **spiritual need** was **to know Jesus as her personal Savior**. To meet this need, Jesus spoke **truth** and used the *common ground of water* to help her recognize her spiritual condition. First, He gave her the opportunity to meet His physical need for water. Next, He offered to meet her spiritual need for *Living Water*, Himself.

To test the honesty and sincerity of her heart, Jesus said, "Go, call your husband and come back." When she responded truthfully that she had no husband, He revealed His divine nature by speaking words of **truth** to her about her previous marriages and current living arrangement. How could a perfect stranger know such things?

Jesus communicated His *love and acceptance* by not being critical and judgmental of her. Though He knew she had had five husbands and was living with a man out of wedlock, He didn't proceed to tell her that she was a bad person or that she needed to change. He already knew her heart; that she was searching and waiting for the Messiah, and that the timing for their conversation was perfect.

Jesus held **truth** up to her like a mirror against which she would see herself clearly. That truth helped her realize that she had been looking in all the wrong places for love. He used dialogue to introduce the Samaritan woman to the One who could meet her need for forgiveness and unconditional love.

OUTCOME OF JESUS' DIALOGUE WITH THE WOMAN AT THE WELL (John 4:28-30, 39-42)

Alive with a new spiritual thirst for Jesus, the Samaritan woman ran into town exclaiming, "Come, see a man who told me everything I ever did. Could this be the Christ?" (John 4:29). The townspeople made their way toward Jesus to see for themselves.

Many of the Samaritans believed in Jesus based solely on the woman's testimony. With a newfound desire to know more about Jesus, they urged Him to spend more time with them. Jesus, always knowing who to stop and make time for, stayed with them for two days. As a result, many more became believers.

"They said to the woman, 'We no longer believe just because of what you said; now we have heard for ourselves, and we know that this man really is the Savior of the world' " (John 4:42).

In what ways do you see *Christlike dialogue* as an effective means of evangelism? Is God nudging you to initiate a life-changing dialogue with someone? With God's help, are you willing to use **grace and truth** to meet that person's **emotional and spiritual needs**?

CHAPTER EIGHTEEN

Life-Changing Dialogue #2

Again Jesus said, "Simon son of John, do you truly love me?"

—John 21:16

There can only be two basic loves, the love of God unto the forgetfulness of self, or the love of self unto the forgetfulness of God.

—Augustine

PETER DENIES KNOWING JESUS (Luke 22:31-34; 54-62)

On that terrible night when Jesus was arrested and tried, Simon Peter denied being Jesus' disciple. He further denied even knowing Jesus. But one morning after the resurrection, Jesus restored the wayward disciple by giving him a chance to reaffirm his love for Christ three times—the same number of times he had denied Him.

Before listening to Jesus' *life-changing dialogue* with Peter, let's first recount Peter's denial of Jesus.

On the day Jesus was arrested for trial, Jesus met with Peter to inform him that Satan had asked to sift Peter as wheat. Jesus encouraged Peter, telling him He had prayed that his faith would not fail. He then instructed Peter to strengthen his brothers, after he had turned back.

Being *self-confident* of his loyalty to Jesus, Peter informed Him that he was ready to go with Him to prison and to death. Knowing better, Jesus told Peter that he would deny knowing Him three times before the rooster would crow that day.

Later that same day, Jesus was taken to the house of the high priest, Caiaphas, for questioning. Peter followed at a distance. After seeing a fire kindled in the courtyard of the high priest, Peter sat down among the servants and officers to wait. A servant girl recognized his face through the light of the fire and pointed out that Peter had been with Jesus.

Not only did Peter deny that he knew Jesus, he told the girl he didn't even understand what she was saying. The first denial had taken place.

A short time later a man saw Peter and accused him of being one of Christ's disciples.

Peter lied again, telling the man he was not one of them—and the second denial was spoken.

After hearing Peter's accent, another bystander contended that Peter must have been with Jesus, because he was a Galilean.

For the third time, Peter had denied knowing Jesus. And just as the words left his mouth, a rooster crowed. At that moment, the Lord turned and looked directly at Peter, a look that Peter would never forget. Immediately, he remembered Jesus' words, "I tell you, Peter, before the rooster crows today, you will deny three times that you know me" (Luke 22:34). But Peter did know Jesus, and because he knew Him his heart was broken. With an overwhelming sense of shame, Peter went outside and wept bitterly.

The denials had taken place. Peter had rejected the One he loved so much—the One he had followed so closely for the past three years—the Person who knew Peter so very well.

Could these spontaneous denials be forgiven? Could the life of a person who so blatantly disowned his Savior, ever again be used for God's glory? Would a person with such weak faith be able to trust Jesus enough to make Him Lord of his life? Could a fearful man such as Peter was that evening, go on to proclaim Jesus Christ with great courage and boldness? Would he have the humility to become a shepherd of God's flock?

It would take a miracle.

AN EARLY MORNING DIALOGUE (John 21:1-19)

After Jesus' resurrection, He appears near the Sea of Tiberias. Peter, James, John, and four other disciples had just spent the night fishing. Early in the morning, the disciples heard a man on shore calling out to them. The man heard that they hadn't caught any fish, so he told them to throw their net on the right side of the boat, which they did. Catching a large number of fish, they realized the man on the shore was Jesus. With excitement, Peter jumped into the water and the others followed by boat.

On shore they saw Jesus tending a fire of burning coals

with fish on it. Handing them some bread, Jesus invited them to join Him for breakfast.

When they had finished eating, a dialogue began between Jesus and Peter:

Jesus: "Simon son of John, do you truly love me more than these?"

Simon Peter: "Yes, Lord," he said, "you know that I love you."

Jesus: "Feed my lambs."

Jesus: "Simon son of John, do you truly love me?"

Simon Peter: "Yes, Lord, you know that I love you."

Jesus: "Take care of my sheep."

Jesus: "Simon son of John, do you love me?"

Simon Peter: "Lord, you know all things; you know that I love you."

Jesus: "Feed my sheep."

Jesus: "I tell you the truth, when you were younger you dressed yourself and went where you wanted; but when you are old you will stretch out your hands, and someone else will dress you and lead you where you do not want to go." Jesus said this to indicate the kind of death by which Peter would glorify God. Then he said to him, "Follow me!"

MEETING PETER'S NEEDS THROUGH GRACE AND TRUTH

It's a simple, yet *life-changing dialogue*. Throughout the conversation, Jesus communicated both **grace and truth** in ways that met the **emotional and spiritual needs** of Peter.

Jesus extended **grace to meet Peter's emotional need for love, acceptance and affirmation**. Here are two ways in which He did so:

- Jesus never mentioned Peter's mistake.
- Jesus asked questions instead of offering criticism.

The first question was, "Do you truly love me more than these?"

Prior to his denials of Jesus, Peter had been self-confident and readily assumed his loyalty to Jesus. He had proclaimed earlier that he would be more devoted than all the other followers of Christ (Matthew 26:33).

So Peter's reply to Jesus, "Yes, Lord, you know that I love you" was confirmation that his self-confidence in his loyalty to Jesus was replaced with humility as he no longer professed to love Jesus more than others.

Jesus asked Peter two more times if he loved Him, not because Jesus needed to know the answer, but because Peter did. Jesus already knew Peter's heart. He had seen his friend weeping bitterly after the rooster had crowed for the third time. But having denied his Savior three times, Peter was likely struggling to trust his own heart, wondering how he could love Jesus, one moment proclaiming that he would die with Him, and denying Him the next. Jesus asked the three questions to help Peter know with certainty that he truly did love Jesus deeply, in spite of the denials.

While listening to Jesus' questions, Peter may have recalled

His Teacher's glance the night before the crucifixion, just as the rooster crowed for the third time. Fresh in Peter's memory was the fact that he saw no disgust or disappointment in the eyes or on the face of His Savior. Instead, he saw what he was in need of at that moment—an expression of compassion and forgiveness—a look that conveyed the message, *"I still love you."*

With three commands, "feed my lambs," "take care of my sheep," and "feed my sheep" Jesus, the Good Shepherd, gave Peter *affirmation* that he was still the right man to serve as a shepherd of God's flock, in spite of the denials. That's **grace**! And through those **words of love—acceptance—and affirmation**, Jesus restored and reinstated Peter to the position He had previously called him to. Through that life-changing dialogue, Jesus enabled Peter to experience the unmerited love of God in a deep, intimate way.

Jesus concludes the dialogue with words of **truth** to meet Peter's **spiritual need of knowing Jesus Christ as Lord of his life**, a Lord who must never again be denied by Peter.

In verses 18-19, Jesus communicated **truth** clearly and directly to Peter. He informed him that the cost of following Jesus would include the loss of his life for the purpose of glorifying God. Then Jesus said, *"Follow me!"*

Jesus used this *life-changing dialogue* to help Peter understand that to follow Jesus in ways that glorify God would require Peter's unswerving loyalty and devotion to His Lord, even when faced with death. And for the rest of his life, Peter persevered in his commission to feed and care for His Lord's sheep, as Jesus had instructed him to do on that early morning by the Sea of Tiberias.

OUTCOME OF JESUS' DIALOGUE WITH PETER

Jesus' tender and thought-provoking dialogue led Peter to know with certainty that Jesus had forgiven him. That assurance would enable Peter to *boldly proclaim truth* to those who had just crucified Christ. With a newly refreshed heart and faith in his Lord, he was prepared to preach these words:

> Men of Israel, listen to this: Jesus of Nazareth was a man accredited by God to you by miracles, wonders and signs, which God did among you through him, as you yourselves know. This man was handed over to you by God's set purpose and foreknowledge; and you, with the help of wicked men, put him to death by nailing him to the cross. But God raised him from the dead...

> Therefore let all Israel be assured of this: God has made this Jesus, whom you crucified, both Lord and Christ.

> When the people heard this, they were cut to the heart and said to Peter and the other apostles, "Brothers, what shall we do?"

> Peter replied, "Repent and be baptized, every one of you, in the name of Jesus Christ for the forgiveness of your sins. And you will receive the gift of the Holy Spirit. The promise is for you and your children and for all who are far off—for all whom the Lord our God will call. (Acts 2:22-24; 36-39)

Three thousand people were saved that day.

161

Do you think Peter would ever have been able to proclaim Christ with such boldness if Jesus had not taken the time to meet Peter's **emotional** and **spiritual needs** through **grace** and **truth** on that early morning by the sea?

And as He did with Peter, Jesus poses the same question to us, *"Do you love Me?"*

In John 14:15, Jesus tells us that if we love Him, we will obey His command. And in John 15:12 we learn that Jesus' command is that we love each other as He has loved us.

In what ways are you loving others as Christ has loved you?

As you prepare to initiate dialogue with someone with an opposing view, will you seek to meet his needs, rather than attempt to change his mind?

Will you pray and ask God to enable you, through the power of His Holy Spirit, to extend grace to meet the person's emotional need for love, acceptance and affirmation? Will you ask God to help you speak words of truth to meet the individual's need to know Jesus Christ as his personal Savior and Lord?

CHAPTER NINETEEN

Evangelistic Listening

My dear brothers, take note of this: Everyone should be quick to listen, slow to speak and slow to become angry, for man's anger does not bring about the righteous life that God desires.

If anyone considers himself religious and yet does not keep a tight rein on his tongue, he deceives himself and his religion is worthless.

—James 1:19-20, 26

We must regularly ask ourselves if our conversations live up to the servant attitude of Jesus. Do we take the time to understand what others are trying to tell us? Do we care enough to listen?

Listening displays the opposite of selfishness because it makes another person more important than ourselves. Any such act of humility allows the character of Jesus to grow in our lives. Conversely, any act of pride stunts that growth.

It's only as we take the time to listen to people that we will begin to understand why they speak and act the way they do.

Are we willing to take that time?

Jesus did. With the Samaritan woman in the middle of the day. With Nicodemus in the middle of the night. And with us whenever we've needed to talk.

Do we really want to be like Jesus?

163

That's the *real* question, isn't it?

For if we become like Him, it will change not only the way we live; it will change the way we listen.

—John Vawter, *Uncommon Graces*, pp. 44-45, 56

POINTING PEOPLE TO JESUS

A pastor was aware of a New Age bookstore in his community that had a coffee shop inside. He saw it as a great opportunity to get acquainted with people who had not yet come to a saving knowledge of Jesus Christ and to work on preparing his sermon.

One day, as he was about to leave the bookstore, he approached the checkout counter and asked the clerk, "What is your opinion of Christians?"

As the clerk observed the pastor's Bible, his response to the question was, "Oh, they're okay; they're fine."

Convinced he hadn't heard the truth, the pastor pushed his Bible and study books aside, looked the clerk in the eyes, and asked, "Now, what do you really think of Christians?"

This time the clerk gave his honest answer: "I think they are rude, arrogant, judgmental, inconsiderate, and they treat me like I'm a bad person."

The pastor replied, "Jesus isn't like that." He then began to share with the clerk how Jesus treated the Samaritan woman at the well, the woman caught in adultery, and the sinful woman who anointed Jesus' feet with her tears, as told in Luke 7:36-50.

The pastor explained that Jesus didn't turn them away because they were sinners. Instead, He loved and accepted them by speaking the truth in love, while never condoning their sin.

Excited by this new revelation, the clerk told the pastor

that the owner of the bookstore, who was also a city councilman, needed to hear that message. Later that day, the clerk gave the pastor's telephone number to his boss.

Early the next morning, the owner of the bookstore called the pastor and asked if he would meet him for breakfast at 7:30 a.m.

The pastor rearranged his schedule to meet with the owner. For two hours, the pastor *listened* attentively while the owner shared his negative views of Christians. When the man finished talking, the pastor replied, "Jesus isn't like that." He went on to share Jesus' love and acceptance of the sinful woman who wiped His feet with her tears.

After their dialogue, the pastor invited the man to a Sunday service at his church and asked if he would share with the entire congregation his thoughts on how people claiming to be Christians are perceived by people who are not Christians.

The man accepted the invitation, and on that Sunday he addressed the entire congregation. When he finished sharing, the pastor laid his arm around the man's shoulder and prayed for him. With tears in his eyes, the councilman looked out at the congregation and said, "If all of you would treat people in this city the way your pastor has treated me, you could turn this city around."

He added, "In forty some years, not one person has ever invited me to church, until your pastor invited me here today."

May our hearts be broken over the lack of Christlike love and concern we demonstrate toward people who do not know Jesus Christ and His incomprehensible love for people.

CULTIVATING A CULTURE OF OTHER-MINDED LISTENING

How will others be drawn to Christ if they observe Christians responding self-righteously over issues such as abortion, sexual immorality, and even prayer? What kind of witness do Christians have as the world takes note of how many of our marriages end in divorce? What kind of appeal do our churches have to spiritual seekers if we are always quarreling over local church practices or denominational differences?

The problem is that we're not listening to others. We're talking. Wouldn't it be wonderful if the body of Christ were known and respected as being excellent *listeners*, rather than stereotyped as close-minded right-wingers?

The city councilman in the story made the comment, "If all of you would treat people in this city the way your pastor has treated me, you could turn this city around."

How did the pastor treat the man? Without ever saying so, the pastor showed the man that all Christians are not as the councilman perceived them to be. He modeled *Christlikeness* in the following ways:

1. He communicated **grace** by *asking questions and listening* to meet the man's **emotional need** for love, acceptance, and affirmation.

2. He communicated **truth** to meet his **spiritual need** to know Jesus by saying, "Jesus isn't like that" and using the Word of God to explain and confirm what Jesus is like.

Just think of the powerful witness God's people can have for Christ if we begin seeing disagreements and controversial issues as opportunities to practice and model *Christlike civility*. As we humbly and *graciously listen* to people with opposing views, and then *speak the truth in love*, we communicate in ways that honor and glorify God.

Would people who know *you,* acknowledge that you are a good listener? If not, are you willing to practice and become an excellent other-minded listener?

PART SIX

Becoming An Answer To God's Call

CHAPTER TWENTY

Insight Into Christlike Dialogue

That the life of Jesus also may be manifested in our body.

—2 Corinthians 4:10, NASB

Remember that you have been saved so that the life of Jesus may be manifested in your body.

You did not do anything to achieve your salvation, but you must do something to exhibit it. You must "work *out* your own salvation" which God has worked *in* you already (Philippians 2:12). Are your speech, your thinking, and your emotions evidence that you are working it "out"?

—Oswald Chambers, *My Utmost for His Highest*, May 15

If Christians truly desire to replace gossip and quarreling with communication that is honoring to God, they will engage in Christlike dialogue. This chapter lists some of the characteristics and benefits of this kind of communication. Take note that the characteristics listed are also attributes of spiritual maturity. As we mature in Christ through the practice of dialoguing with others as Jesus did, we will experience the blessings and benefits of Christlike dialogue.

CHARACTERISTICS OF CHRISTLIKE DIALOGUE

1. People stop being too busy, and become available to build relationships with God and with people through dialogue. (Luke 10:25-42)

2. Selfish ambition is replaced with other-mindedness. (Philippians 2:3-4)

3. People are slow to speak and quick to listen. (James 1:19-20)

4. People obey Christ's command to love others as He has loved us by:

   a. Accepting one another. (Romans 15:7)
   b. Bearing with and forgiving one another. (Colossians 3:13)
   c. Laying down our lives for one another. (1 John 3:16)
   d. Serving one another. (John 13:1-17)
   e. Suffering injustice. (1 Peter 2:18-23; 4:1-2)
   f. Extending grace, kindness and mercy to others. (Titus 3:3-7)

5. People speak words of grace to convey love, acceptance and affirmation of others, and words of truth that point people to Jesus Christ and the Word of God. (John 1:17)

6. Words are spoken with humility and respect for others, while Jesus Christ and the Word of God are proclaimed boldly. (Acts 28:31; 1 Peter 3:15)

7. Evidence that we are being conformed to the likeness of Christ becomes more obvious as:

   a. Quarreling is replaced with peaceful conversation. (2 Timothy 2:24)
   b. People treat one another with kindness. (2 Timothy 2:24)
   c. We gently instruct one another. (2 Timothy 2:25)

8. The presence of the Holy Spirit is evident, and conversations are honoring to God. (2 Corinthians 3:17-18)

9. God's people become known by our Christlike love for one another. (John 13:34-35)

Those *characteristics* of Christlike dialogue are representative of the nature and attributes of Jesus Christ and the fruit of His Spirit that become evident in the lives of Christians as we abide in Christ and walk in His Spirit.

The potential *benefits* of Christlike dialogue listed on pages 174-175 can become reality through application of the biblical principles written in this book.

POTENTIAL BENEFITS OF CHRISTLIKE DIALOGUE

1. God's people will experience a deeper level of spiritual maturity as we grow in our knowledge of the Son of God. (Romans 12:1-2; Ephesians 4:13)

   a. Individuals discover significant meaning and purpose for living as they apply the biblical principles for Christlike dialogue.

2. Individuals respond as Christ would to people of opposing views. (John 1:17; Ephesians 4:15; 2 Timothy 2:24-25)

   a. Husbands and wives, parents and children enjoy peaceful conversations.

   b. Young people have healthy dialogues with parents and peers as they search for truth in regard to life's challenges.

   c. Christians bear witness unto Jesus Christ as we practice *Christlike civility* when discussing controversial issues.

3. Unity occurs within the body of Christ as we keep a single-minded focus on Christ and His interests. (Psalm 133:1; John 17:20-23; Romans 15:5-7; Philippians 2:21)

   a. Congregations are transformed as gossip and quarreling are replaced with Christlike dialogue.

b. Church leadership has peaceful and productive communication amongst themselves, and with laity.

c. Ministry teams work together more efficiently and effectively as they cultivate environments of listening and other-mindedness.

4. Unbelievers are drawn to Jesus and God is glorified as they witness God's people having sincere Christlike love for one another. (Matthew 5:13a, 14a, 16)

DIFFERENCES BETWEEN DEBATE AND DIALOGUE

	DEBATE	CHRISTLIKE DIALOGUE
Goal	Win the argument	Mature in Christ for God's glory
Motive	To be "right"	To do right by loving others as Christ has loved you
Format	Statements	Questions and statements
Listening	Only to counter opposing views	To learn from one another, and to better understand each other

Knowledge	Used proudly to prove superiority of intellect	Used humbly as a gift to share and to point others to Jesus and the Word of God
Transparency	Unwilling to admit being wrong	Willing to admit being wrong
Mind-Set	Not willing to change	Seeking to become *more like Christ*

True *Christlike dialogue* occurs when both parties surrender all pride and selfish ambition and concentrate on Christ's interests with a desire for God's will to be done for His glory. But even if one of the parties is not willing to surrender, that does not prevent *you* from communicating with *Christlike civility*.

CHAPTER TWENTY-ONE

Guidelines for Initiating Dialogue

May the words of my mouth and the meditation of my heart be pleasing in your sight, O Lord, my Rock and my Redeemer.

—Psalm 19:14

Every man is a potential adversary, even those whom we love. Only through dialogue are we saved from this enmity toward one another. Dialogue is to love, what blood is to the body. When the flow of blood stops, the body dies. When dialogue stops, love dies and resentment and hate are born. But dialogue can restore a dead relationship. Indeed, this is the miracle of dialogue: it can bring relationship into being, and it can bring into being once again a relationship that has died.

There is only one qualification to these claims for dialogue: it must be mutual and proceed from both sides, and the parties to it must persist relentlessly. The word of dialogue may be spoken by one side but evaded or ignored by the other, in which case the promise may not be fulfilled. There is risk in speaking the dialogical word—that is, in entering into dialogue—but when two persons undertake it and accept their fear of doing so, the miracle-working power of dialogue may be released.

—Reuel L. Howe, *The Miracle of Dialogue,* pp. 3-4

PREPARING HEARTS FOR DIALOGUE

This chapter provides guidelines for initiating dialogue with someone who has an opposing view. **The guidelines are offered for the purpose of preparing hearts for Christlike dialogue, rather than as steps to follow.** They also help to establish some parameters.

I encourage you to initiate dialogue in the simplest way possible. In my earlier introduction, I explained how I initiated dialogue with the leader of a secular organization in regard to sex education in the public schools. I simply called her on the telephone and asked if she would be willing to meet with me to dialogue. I explained that my purpose was to see if we could find some common ground and learn together where we disagreed. After accepting my offer, we met and agreed that our common ground was "healthier kids and a healthy society." We decided when and how often we would meet, and then began to dialogue.

Initiating dialogue can be as simple as asking someone if they are willing to dialogue about a concern that you have. If the answer is "Yes.", you have begun.

KEEPING IT SIMPLE

After attending an Accountability Ministries' seminar on *Christlike Dialogue*, a woman initiated dialogue with her sister. One is a Democrat, the other a Republican. She wrote:

> This seminar made me realize that I didn't have to win or change my mind or the other person's mind in order to have a conversation. I also didn't have to lose. It opened me to asking questions and getting another point of view rather than having an agenda.
>
> I found conversing with people now is a lot more

fun, and I can get involved in a conversation where I know people are not on the same side as me. I'm finding that really interesting, and it's stretching me. With this approach, I'm also finding some common ground—for two reasons. First, I'm involved in a conversation that I wouldn't have had, and second, I'm not approaching it as an antagonist. That helps people listen to me because I'm listening to them. It's not magic; it just feels like it. So different than before.

Instead of always being on edge with my sister, I was able to relax and just enjoy all the good things about her. That critical spirit that was often around when we were together wasn't there this time. Instead, it was a spirit of affirmation.

If there is a person in your life with whom you currently have a difference of opinion, I encourage you to pray and ask God if it is His will for you to initiate dialogue with that person. Ask God for His wisdom and blessing before you proceed to initiate dialogue. You want to be certain that God is the One who is leading you to initiate dialogue. If so, invite Him to join you in the conversation.

I urge you to keep in mind the fact that people are at different levels of spiritual maturity. Check the expectations you have of yourself or others to be sure they are realistic. You're not there to change the person to your way of thinking. Remain humble, teachable and open to patiently bearing with others in love. Allow time for the Holy Spirit to work in people's lives, including yours.

Prepare to respond as Christ would, but be equally prepared for others *not to*. Remember that discussing differences of opinion often reveals hearts and how much we have, or have not, grown in grace.

GUIDELINES FOR INITIATING DIALOGUE

The guidelines that follow are for two people who desire to mature in Christ and communicate in ways that are pleasing and honoring to God.

However, *if the partners in a dialogue are not Christians who seek to honor God and mature in Christ, note the difference in wording for numbers two, four, six and seven in italics.* The remaining guidelines stay the same.

1. If one of the parties is in authority over the other, it's important that the person in authority give the one under his authority the freedom to respectfully discuss matters of concern without being criticized or punished for it. (Matthew 20:25-28)

2. Agree on a common goal, namely, "to reach unity in the faith and in the knowledge of the Son of God and become mature, attaining to the whole measure of the fullness of Christ," and to build a relationship that glorifies God. (1 Corinthians 10:31; Ephesians 4:13)

    Agree on a common goal, namely, to discuss differences and come to a knowledge of the truth.

3. Identify a common subject of interest for the dialogue. This does not need to be the issue or concern that you are in disagreement about. It may be anything the parties can identify as *common ground* that might help them build a relationship and accomplish their goal(s). (John 4:7,10,13-14)

4. Prior to the discussion, the two should agree to forgive each other if one offends the other in any way as they

dialogue. Also, they should agree that when they finish, they will love and accept each other even if they still disagree. (Romans 15:7; 1 John 4:19-21)

Prior to the discussion, the two should agree that when they finish their dialogue, they will not be critical or judgmental of each other even if they still disagree.

5. Each person should be open to the possibility of being wrong about their position, and to the possibility of being deceived in certain ways. (Jeremiah 17:9; James 1:26)

6. Prior to beginning each dialogue, agree to pray a prayer along these lines: "Father, whatever is in our lives that You want to take out or change, help us to recognize it and yield to You. Show us the truth. Let us see any deception in our lives that You want us to be free of." (Psalm 139:23-24)

If, during the dialogue, one of the participants recognizes that the Lord is convicting him of something in his life that is wrong, invite your dialogue partner to support your repentance with prayer. Then thank him for being an instrument of the Lord in opening your eyes to the truth.

If both people are willing, pray before each dialogue, asking God to bring each of you to a greater knowledge and understanding of truth.

7. Agree to give one another the freedom to speak the truth in love as each perceives it, without interruption from the other person (except to ask questions for

clarification). The underlying motive must be love for God and love for each other and a desire to learn what changes, if any, God wants either or both parties to make that will help both of them mature in Christ. (Matthew 22:37-39; Ephesians 4:15)

> *Agree to give one another the freedom to speak the truth in love as each perceives it, without interruption from the other person, except to ask questions for clarification. Furthermore, be open to replacing your opinion of truth with the real truth if either of you are proved wrong.*

8. Listen and learn from each other but don't attempt to persuade the other person to your point of view or assume the other is wrong just because he or she doesn't agree with you. (Proverbs 18:13; James 1:19-20)

9. It's not important that you agree with each other. What is important is that you agree with God, mature in Christ, and maintain love and respect for each other despite differences. (1 Peter 2:17)

10. The two should agree to leave the other person's decision, and consequences of that decision, between the person and God, unless church discipline needs to be properly administered in love by following the principles in Matthew 18:15-17.

11. Close by praying and asking God to grant both of you repentance as needed, leading whomever is deceived to a knowledge of the truth for God's glory and their

well-being. (2 Timothy 2:25)

—Jeff Rosenau, *Building Bridges Not Walls,*
NavPress, pp. 129-132 (paraphrased)

With whom has God been leading *you* to initiate dialogue?

CHAPTER TWENTY-TWO

Are You Approachable?

Jesus called them together and said, "You know that the rulers of the Gentiles lord it over them, and their high officials exercise authority over them. Not so with you."

—Matthew 20:25-26

Godly leaders...are free of the need to *lord it over people.* Beware of any Christian movement in which the leader must always be first, must always be in charge, must always be right.

—Center for Church Based Training, *Church Leadership Series: the Leader,* p. 9

The first guideline for initiating dialogue on page 180 states that if one of the parties is in authority over the other, it's important that the person in authority give the one under his or her authority the freedom to discuss matters of concern as long as they do so respectfully.

The intent of this guideline is to grant the person under authority permission and freedom to share their concerns openly, without being criticized or punished for it. Without this security, leadership would seldom learn how they and/or their decisions impact those under their authority.

Many homes, churches and businesses operate far less efficiently, effectively, and peacefully than possible when leadership fails to listen to the creative, beneficial ideas and insights that those under their authority are more than willing to share, if given the opportunity.

Leaders may also be unaware of certain weaknesses or character flaws that don't fit with their testimony as Christians, but are clearly evident to those around them, unless they give those under their authority permission to respectfully talk about them with their leader in helpful, constructive, "iron sharpens iron" ways (Proverbs 27:17). The leader is then free to accept their comments as being true, or to reject them as being inaccurate, hopefully after giving prayerful consideration to what has been noted.

FREEDOM TO CONFRONT

By way of illustration, let me tell you about my two wonderful sons, Rob and Travis. They are grown up now, but when they were young I gave them the *freedom to confront* me when they thought I was wrong, as long as they did so *respectfully*.

Once or twice a year, I would ask them, "What don't you like about me as a dad?" and "How can I be a better dad?"

My oldest son Rob once replied, "You're an over-thinker

and an over-planner."

Impressed by my son's honest and accurate answer, I said, "Thank you, Rob. I am an over-thinker and an over-planner, so hopefully your reminder will help me loosen up and live a day at a time." More recently my son's comment reminded me to think less, plan less, and pray more.

When my sons were home on summer vacation from college, one of God's greatest blessings was the privilege of working outdoors with Rob and Travis in our seasonal job of adjusting property insurance claims. We were a team and each of us had separate, supportive roles and responsibilities. One evening on our way home from a hard day's work, I asked again, "What don't you like about me as a dad?" and "How can I be a better dad?"

This time they respectfully implied that I was a controller and had not given them much say about their choice of roles while on the job. As they had several years of experience and did excellent work, that night I gave them the responsibility of deciding each person's role for the next day. I suggested that they choose their own assignments, assuming the role they felt most qualified to do and enjoyed the most. I also gave them permission to delegate the job assignment I should have. The next day was most enjoyable for everyone and turned out to be even more efficient than our previous arrangement.

Another lesson learned.

One day as I was riding in the car with my youngest son Travis, we had a little difference of opinion. As we talked, I began to realize that he was right and I was wrong, so I said, "I was wrong, but..."

No sooner had the word "but" left my mouth, when Travis boldly replied, "Dad, no 'buts.' I just want to hear you say these three words, 'I was wrong.' "

I looked over at my son, smiled, and said, "Travis, I was

wrong." I thanked him for the accountability as I had obviously tried to justify myself, but couldn't.

Those three words—**"I WAS WRONG"**—are powerful. They can restore marriages and keep churches from splitting. They can even prevent wars between countries. But they have this effect only if people in authority are willing to say them with sincerity.

A LOOK IN THE MIRROR

Are you a person in authority? Do you give those under your authority the freedom to confront you if they do so respectfully?

Are you an over-thinker or over-planner—too often giving priority to tasks rather than people and relationships? Are you too controlling—always demanding that things be done your way without considering input from those under your authority? When you have made a mistake and are wrong, are you willing to acknowledge it?

If you allow others the freedom to confront you respectfully, you may become aware of weaknesses that can adversely affect the lives of others as well as your Christian witness. If that is the case, would you not welcome the truth if it is spoken in love?

I praise God for the relationship my sons and I have and the freedom we've given each other to speak the truth in love to one another, but I realize many husbands, parents, pastors, employers, and world leaders fail to give people under their authority freedom to disagree, even if done so in a respectful way. Let's pray that this will change.

The following are questions you, as a person in authority over another, can ask people such as your spouse, children, employees, staff and laity, as the Holy Spirit leads you:

- What weaknesses do you see in my life that are keeping me from being a more godly spouse, parent, employer, pastor, or friend?

- What character qualities or habits of mine offend you, and what changes would you like to see in me that can improve our relationship?

When you are ready to open the door for such open and honest dialogue, I encourage you to invite the Holy Spirit to guide you in your conversations. Ask God for His wisdom, His words, spoken in His Spirit, in order that these conversations might be occasions in which the truth is spoken *in love*.

Be on guard against these two barriers to dialogue that were addressed in chapters three and four:

Selfish Ambition
Busyness

Don't let these barriers keep you from initiating and engaging others in *Christlike dialogue*. And may you and the person you talk with *come to know Jesus Christ more intimately* as you communicate in ways that are pleasing and honoring to God.

Conclusion

Are You Living for Jesus?

For Christ's love compels us, because we are convinced that one died for all, and therefore all died. And he died for all, that those who live should no longer live for themselves but for him who died for them and was raised again.

—2 Corinthians 5:14-15

Christianity is not a set of teachings to understand. It is a Person to follow.

—Dr. Henry Blackaby,
Experiencing God Day by Day, Back Cover

WILL *YOU* BE AN ANSWER TO GOD'S CALL?

I pray that each person who reads this book will become an answer to God's call for His children to *grow up into the likeness of His Son,* so much so, that we communicate with and respond to people of opposing views with a *Christlike civility* that glorifies God.

Do you recall the reason for the emphasis on communication? Because the words we speak reveal our hearts. How has God been speaking to *your heart* while reading this book?

Do you remember the results of the survey from the quiz presented in chapter one, revealing that gossip, quarreling, stereotyping and apathy are far more prevalent among God's people than dialogue in the Spirit of Christ?

Think back to Dr. Blackaby's questions:

- Are we going to be a people like God has asked us to be?
- Will we stop fussing within our churches?
- Will we stop fussing between our churches?
- Will we ask God to give us one heart and one mind and one soul?

Just think of the impact Christians can have on society if we practice and model *Christlike civility* by communicating in ways that please, honor and glorify God.

Will we respond with Christlike civility in the midst of conflict? Will we be a people known by our love for one another? Are we willing to repent of our conformity to this world and ready to be transformed into the likeness of Christ by the renewing of our minds?

Will *you* respond to our heavenly Father's challenge to become more and more like Christ in the ways you speak to others, especially those with opposing views?

God has given us everything we need to be less like this

world, and more like His Son.

> His divine power has given us everything we need
> for life and godliness through our knowledge of
> him who called us by his own glory and goodness.
> Through these he has given us his very great and
> precious promises, so that through them you may
> participate in the divine nature and escape the
> corruption in the world caused by evil desires.
>
> For this very reason, make every effort to add to
> your faith goodness; and to goodness, knowledge;
> and to knowledge, self-control; and to self-control,
> perseverance; and to perseverance, godliness; and to
> godliness, brotherly kindness; and to brotherly
> kindness, love. For if you possess these qualities in
> increasing measure, they will keep you from being
> ineffective and unproductive in your knowledge of
> our Lord Jesus Christ. (2 Peter 1:3-8)

Dear Heavenly Father, I pray that Your Holy Spirit will use the words in this book to touch the hearts and transform the lives of Your children. May Your Holy Spirit bring conviction of how we fall short of heeding Your call to communicate with *Christlike civility* when responding to people who disagree with us. Grant us repentance that leads to change; change that is pleasing and honoring to You. And Father, I ask that You will use *When Christians Act Like Christians* to help the body of Christ to grow in our knowledge of Your Son so that our relationship with Him will enable us to respond to people of opposing views with a *Christlike civility* that draws others to Jesus Christ, for Your glory.

Dear reader, will *you* be an answer to God's call?

ENDNOTES

The following are the sources of excerpts used in this book:

Chapter One: I AM A CHRISTIAN, BUT AM I ACTING CHRISTLIKE?

1. Billy Graham, *The Journey* (Nashville, TN: W Publishing Group, a division of Thomas Nelson, Inc., 2006), 78-79.

Chapter Two: IS MY GOAL TO BE "RIGHT", OR TO DO RIGHT?

2. Oswald Chambers, *My Utmost for His Highest* (Grand Rapids, MI: Discovery House Publishers, 1992), May 6.

3. Paul David Tripp, *War of Words: Getting to the Heart of Your Communication Struggles* (Phillipsburg, NJ: P&R Publishing Company, 2000), 7.

4. David C. Reardon, *Making Abortion Rare: A Healing Strategy for a Divided Nation* (Springfield, IL: Acorn, 1996), 6.

Chapter Three: SELF-CENTERED, OR OTHER-MINDED?

5. Dr. Emerson Eggerichs, *Love & Respect* (Nashville, TN: Thomas Nelson, Inc., 2004), 6.

Chapter Four: TOO BUSY, OR AVAILABLE?

6. Bill Hybels, *Too Busy Not to Pray*, 2nd ed. (Downers Grove, IL: InterVarsity Press, 1998), 125-126, 147.

7. J. Oswald Sanders, *Spiritual Leadership* (Chicago, IL: The Moody Bible Institute, 1994), 96.

Chapter Five: TRANSFORMING POWER OF THE HOLY SPIRIT

8. W. Glyn Evans, *Daily with my Lord* (Chicago, IL: The Moody Bible Institute, 1999), August 20.

Chapter Six: CONFLICT OFFERS OPPORTUNITY

9. Paul David Tripp, *War of Words: Getting to the Heart of Your Communication Struggles* (Phillipsburg, NJ: P&R Publishing Company, 2000), 80.

10. Oswald Chambers, *My Utmost for His Highest* (Grand Rapids, MI: Discovery House Publishers, 1992), February 8.

Chapter Seven: WHAT DOES CHRISTLIKE LOOK LIKE?

11. Oswald Chambers, *My Utmost for His Highest* (Uhrichsville, OH: Barbour Publishing, Inc., 1963), May 11.

12. Rick Warren, *The Purpose Driven Life* (Grand Rapids, MI: Zondervan, 2002), 275-276.

13. Ken Sande, *The Peacemaker* (Grand Rapids, MI: Baker Book House, 1997), 202-203.

Chapter Eight: THE MEEK SURRENDER, BUT NEVER LOSE

14. Richard A. Swenson, M.D., *Margin* (Colorado Springs, CO: NavPress, 1992), 233-234.

15. Oswald Chambers, *My Utmost for His Highest* (Grand Rapids, MI: Discovery House Publishers, 1992), May 6.

16. Roy Hession, *The Calvary Road* (London: Christian Literature Crusade, 1950), 98-101.

Chapter Nine: WHY ARGUING MAY BE OKAY, BUT QUARRELING ISN'T

17. John Vawter, *Uncommon Graces* (Colorado Springs, CO: NavPress, 1998), 116-117.

18. Oxford University Press, Inc., *Oxford American Dictionary* (New York, NY: Oxford University Press, 1980), 32, 547.

Chapter Ten: BE KIND TO WHOM?

19. Andrew Murray, *Abiding in Christ* (Bloomington, MN: Bethany House Publishers, 2003), 161.

Chapter Eleven: WHY ARE WE TO RESPOND GENTLY?

20. Charles R. Swindoll, *Improving Your Serve* (Waco, TX: Word, Incorporated, 1981), 66-67.

Chapter Twelve: ABOVE ALL ELSE, CONTINUE IN
LOVE

21. Andrew Murray, *Absolute Surrender* (Springdale, PA: Whitaker House, 1981, 1982), 35-36.

Chapter Thirteen: JESUS' FORCEFUL RESPONSE TO
THE MONEYCHANGERS

22. John MacArthur, *The MacArthur Study Bible* (Nashville, TN: Word Publishing, 1997), 1579.

Chapter Fourteen: JESUS' JUDGMENTAL WORDS TO
THE PHARISEES

23. Oswald Chambers, *My Utmost for His Highest* (Grand Rapids, MI: Discovery House Publishers, 1992), June 17.

Chapter Fifteen: PAUL ARGUED BOLDLY, BUT WHAT
DID HE ARGUE ABOUT?

24. Andrew Murray, *Abiding in Christ* (Bloomington, MN: Bethany House Publishers, 2003), 122-123.

Chapter Sixteen: THE NEED FOR GRACE AND TRUTH

25. Randy Alcorn, *The Grace and Truth Paradox* (Sisters, OR: Multnomah Publishers, Inc., 2003), 18, 20, 87-88, 92.

Chapter Seventeen: LIFE-CHANGING DIALOGUE #1

26. Philip Yancey, *What's So Amazing About Grace?* (Grand Rapids, MI: Zondervan Publishing House, 1997), 175.

Chapter Nineteen: EVANGELISTIC LISTENING

27. John Vawter, *Uncommon Graces* (Colorado Springs, CO: NavPress, 1998), 44-45, 56.

Chapter Twenty: INSIGHT INTO CHRISTLIKE
DIALOGUE

28. Oswald Chambers, *My Utmost for His Highest* (Grand Rapids, MI: Discovery House Publishers, 1992), May 15.

Chapter Twenty-One: GUIDELINES FOR INITIATING
DIALOGUE

29. Reuel L. Howe, *The Miracle of Dialogue* (Minneapolis, MN: The Seabury Press, Incorporated, 1963), 3-4.

30. Jeff Rosenau, *Building Bridges Not Walls* (Colorado Springs, CO: NavPress, 2003), 129-132.

Chapter Twenty-Two: ARE YOU APPROACHABLE?

31. Center for Church Based Training, *Church Leadership Series: The Leader* (Richardson, TX: Center for Church Based Training, 2005), 9.

Conclusion: ARE YOU LIVING FOR JESUS?

32. Henry T. Blackaby & Richard Blackaby, *Experiencing God Day By Day* (Nashville, TN: B & H Publishing Group, 2006), Back cover.

ABOUT THE AUTHOR

Jeff Rosenau is the founder and president of Accountability Ministries, a Colorado-based organization which began in 1990. Jeff teaches biblical principles that help prepare God's people to *become the people God is calling us to be* by growing in our knowledge of the Son of God so that our relationship with Him will enable us to respond as Jesus would to people of opposing views. He has made numerous presentations for churches, as well as para-church organizations, including Advocates International, Christian Legal Society, Colorado Christian University, Pregnancy Care Centers, Denver Seminary, International Student Connection, Peacemaker Ministries, The Christian and Missionary Alliance, The Navigators, and World Venture. Jeff is the author of *Building Bridges Not Walls: Learning to Dialogue in the Spirit of Christ* (NavPress – 2003), and *Christlike Dialogue* (Accountability Ministries – 2001). He and his wife Candy reside in Centennial, Colorado.

God recently opened doors for Jeff to share internationally with seminary students and Brazilian pastors in Teresina, Brazil, and with law students at Handong International Law School in Pohang, South Korea.

You can contact Jeff in any of the following ways:

Write: **Accountability Ministries**
         7622 South Ivanhoe Way
         Centennial, Colorado 80112

Call: 303-668-8124

E-Mail: jlr@accountabilityministries.org

Web: www.accountabilityministries.org.

NOTES

NOTES

NOTES

NOTES

NOTES

NOTES

CPSIA information can be obtained
at www.ICGtesting.com
Printed in the USA
BVHW030157250219
541072BV00001B/34/P